"This book is the  complains that American teens don't have many ...ell or that they don't have many ... essays, stories, poetry and art in ... ough fresh and unspoiled eyes."

Charles Osgood
television and radio commentator
host, *CBS Sunday Morning*

"Today's young people have so much to say to one another. I applaud *Teen Ink* for providing a forum for their voices."

Lois Lowry
author, *The Giver*

"After reading *Teen Ink,* I truly believe that we are all connected in life through experiences."

Katherine Ryder, age 18

"Real: That is what *Teen Ink* is. All of the thoughts and emotions come from teens brave enough to put their true emotions on paper!"

Greg Pascale, age 14

"What I read in these pages is lifesaving stuff. Not only is much of it astonishingly good from a craft point of view, but it gives teenagers *voice.* In a culture where adolescents are often ignored or treated as second-class citizens, *Teen Ink* gives them a place to say loud and clear who they are."

Chris Crutcher
author, *Staying Fat for Sarah Byrnes* and *Whale Talk*

"*Teen Ink* covers subjects to which any teenager can relate."

Boston Herald

"*Teen Ink* is a remarkable display of the talents, experiences, and views of a generation. The stories, poems and artwork will stir the hearts of the young and old alike. Every teenager should have a copy of this phenomenal publication."

Veronica Lindsay, age 16

"Teen Ink gives me the inspiration to make it through the day. It shows that anyone, no matter what your grades are, can excel in life. It also gives teens a chance to share their opinions, talents and feelings. It gives us the chance to connect with each other and ourselves."

Monica Henry, age 18

"Teen Ink gives meaningful glimpses into the private lives of young adults and shows their triumphs and struggles in their own words."

School Library Journal

"You don't need to be a teenager to benefit from the passion and intelligence flowing from the prose, poetry and artwork in this inspiring collection."

Parenting Today's Teens.com

"Teen Ink has something for every teen. The stories can make you laugh or make you cry, but most of all, they make you feel as though you aren't alone."

Jenny Elliot, age 17

"In case you're needing reassurance . . . that today's young people care about our society, possess inquiring minds and have much to give creatively, *Teen Ink* should give you plenty of comfort."

designer, publication of University and College Designers Association

"When I read *Teen Ink,* I cannot only hear the words but see them in my head, so it is not only a story but a beautiful picture."

Christina Svenningsen, age 14

"Teen Ink has teens telling it like it is."

Wellesley [MA] Townsman

"Heartfelt stories from teens to teens . . . 'nuf said."

Graham Caulkins, age 15

Friends and Family

Edited by
Stephanie H. Meyer
John Meyer

Health Communications, Inc.
Deerfield Beach, Florida

www.hci-online.com
www.TeenInk.com

The following pieces were originally published by The Young Authors Foundation, Inc. (©1989–2001) in *The 21st Century/Teen Ink* magazine. We gratefully acknowledge the many individuals who granted us permission to reprint the cited material.

"Three Friends." Reprinted by permission of Samantha Finigan. ©2001 Samantha Finigan.

"Torrie, Jay and Me." Reprinted by permission of Elisabeth Hansen. ©2001 Elisabeth Hansen.

(continued on page 343)

Library of Congress Cataloging-in-Publication Data

Teen Ink: friends and family / edited by Stephanie H. Meyer, John Meyer.

    p.   cm.

    Summary: A collection of stories and poems by teenage writers, arranged in such categories as "Snapshots: Friends and Family," "Out of Focus: Facing Challenges," and "Candids: Everyday Experiences."

    ISBN 1-55874-931-4 (trade paper)

    1. Adolescence—Literary collections. 2. Youths' writings, American. [1. Adolescence—Literary collections. 2. Youths' writings.] I. Title: Teen Ink friends and family. II. Meyer, Stephanie H., date. III. Meyer, John, date. IV. Teen Ink.

PZ5 .T29495 2001
810.8'09283—dc21

2001039316

Publisher: Health Communications, Inc.
      3201 S.W. 15th Street
      Deerfield Beach, FL 33442-8190

Cover illustration and design by Larissa Hise Henoch
Inside book design by Lawna Patterson Oldfield
Inside book formatting by Dawn Grove

"It is only with the heart that one can see rightly; what is essential is invisible to the eye."

—ANTOINE DE SAINT-EXUPÉRY

To our close friends and family
And the families of writers and artists
who made this book possible

Contents

3. Candids: Everyday Experiences

4. Portraits: Of Moms and Dads

5. Passports: Finding New Places

6. Landscapes: Stories of Grandparents

7. Double Exposures: Changes in Our Lives

8. Close-Ups: Revisiting Our Memories

Preface

by Amber Bard

Our generation has been branded a mess—high on sex, drugs and violence. Read any newspaper, and the headlines scream of the latest teenager gone astray. The articles overflow with musing expert analysis, reducing kids and their problems to coffee-table chitchat. Images of weapon-wielding children playing dictator over their cowering classmates make adults struggle to figure out what went wrong. While psychologists and journalists scribble on notebooks with knitted brows, teens across America are neither brooding over the bad nor basking in the good, but rather contemplating all aspects of life. And, more important, they are preserving these invaluable thoughts in diaries, Web pages, 'zines and here—in *Teen Ink*'s third book in its series of teenage writing.

These books, completely authored by teens like you and me—not annoying adults—take giant strides in the movement to give us a voice with which we can shout to the world. Over a hundred entries freshly document our experiences with friends and enemies, family and strangers.

Whether you paint your toes to *NSync or rock out to the Ramones, prefer Magic Markers to Picasso, shop at

Salvation Army or The Gap, this book represents you—your feelings, your aspirations, your pain. And as a collection of some of the finest writing from teenagers in America today, *Teen Ink: Friends and Family* delivers.

Each piece has been experienced by a real person; the smiles, the tears, the disappointments are all genuine. Even in the fiction pieces, traces of the authors' vulnerabilities and experiences are bright and plentiful.

As every new author knows, writing is more contagious than a cold before an important date. If you gain nothing else from this book, gain the desire to write—to stay up all night, feverishly scrawling thoughts. Gain the desire to scream your words into the ear of every passing person, to stand up and make others listen, to "make things happen."

Prove the cynical critics wrong. Prove to them that the new generation of teenagers are not lazy couch-mongers, but intelligent and progressive people ready to start ironing out the country's problems.

Let the raw words from this book envelop your mind with their creeping tendrils and inspire you to take action. Let the soulful stories and poems inspire you—inspire you to write, inspire you to speak, and inspire you simply "to live."

Amber Bard, a high-school junior, has been published in Teen Ink *magazine, and her poem, "Ohio," is on page 95.*

Introduction

Teen Ink: Friends and Family is the third book in the Teen Ink series and is the next exciting step in presenting and honoring the writing and art of teenagers. Our first two books were compilations of the voices and visions of teens exploring the broadest range of issues, experiences and creativity. And, as with all the books in our series, these authors are all young people whose works have been published in Teen Ink's national monthly magazine during the past twelve years.

After reading more than 300,000 teen submissions since the late eighties, it is clear that teens, like the rest of us, care the most about friends and family, which is reflected here in their prose, poetry and artwork. This shouldn't surprise us since what is more central, more important and, at times, more painful than our friends and family? Who hasn't felt the sting of a friend's anger, the exhilaration of that special moment with a parent or the pain of losing a grandparent? Who has not been blessed with at least one good friend, the love of a sibling or family member, or the warmth of an older person's understanding?

Teens feel deeply, passionately and honestly about all these relationships, often speaking in a louder voice and more candidly than most adults. Teenagers are at a stage where they need to share, need to feel important and unique, and what better way to fill this need than through their words. *Teen Ink: Friends and Family* provides this opportunity for all of us to learn from these gifted and courageous writers and artists who remind us how much young people have to offer, if we are only willing to listen. The power of these voices may at times leave you breathless, or even in tears, as you recall that similar moment in your own life, but you will always be in awe of their amazing ability to add insight and perspective.

We are all bound together in an elaborate web of friends and family, with just "six degrees of separation," and these teens help guide us through its intricacies. We have divided the book into various chapters based on photographic images and exposures. We believe that as you read these pages, clear visions will emerge that represent familiar and unfamiliar landscapes. You will discover an entire family and friends album unfolding within you as these authors reveal their mental pictures for us to develop and process within our own experiences.

We hope you will find pieces in this volume that speak to you, whether you are a teenager, a parent trying to better understand your adolescent, an aunt or uncle trying to become closer to that special niece or nephew, or a grandparent who only wants to know how to communicate better with that odd creature you see periodically but love continually.

We, as parents ourselves, have gained enormously from our own friends and family through times of triumph and tragedy. And we are also enriched by the writings from teens across the country as they continue to share their feelings and submit their work to our magazine and for future books in this series. Their insights reinforce our belief that this country has a very bright future since these young adults already have revealed such a unique understanding of what it's like to be a friend and family member. We again want to thank all the teens who have shared their stories, whether published or not. We only hope that more and more of you will open your hearts and minds to those who love you most—*your* friends and family.

Stephanie H. Meyer
John Meyer

Welcome

This is your book. All the words and images were created by teens and gathered from works that appeared in *Teen Ink* magazine during the last decade.

You can join these teenagers by sending us *your* stories, poems, art and photography to be considered for the monthly *Teen Ink* magazine and future books in this series.

If you want to participate, see the submission guidelines on pages 311–312. You can e-mail your work to us at *editor@TeenInk.com* or mail submissions to Teen Ink, Box 97, Newton, MA 02461.

To learn more about the magazine and to request a free sample copy, see our Web site at *www.TeenInk.com*.

Snapshots:
Friends and Family

Photo by Samantha Finigan

Torrie, Jay and Me

by Elisabeth Hansen

Do you want to go on the seesaw? I bet you haven't done that in years."

Fragments of light glistened through the black abyss, the moon providing just enough to make everything glow. A bitter wind swept through me. It was hard to believe gleeful children had occupied this playground earlier that day. Everything seemed utterly lifeless.

Lifeless . . . The word echoed through my mind.

Don't die, sweet Torrie, not now.

What the heck, I thought and followed Jay across the schoolyard toward the seesaws. My feet sank deep into the pebbles. There was something very nostalgic about the moment, as if I were six years old again.

Jay held his end of the seesaw steady so I could get on. He mounted and situated himself so he almost looked distinguished, but that only lasted a moment. Our weight difference caused me to fly upward, and Jay landed on the ground with a thud.

"That was classic. Where's a camera when you need one?" I joked.

Jay pushed off the ground, and I gradually floated back down. Unexpectedly, I began drifting upward again. I looked at the ground that should have been under my feet, but there was just air. Jay's legs were too long, or maybe mine were too short. Nothing about that moment seemed real. I almost forgot why I was even there with Jay. He wanted to cheer me up, to take my mind off the accident.

I'm sorry I didn't keep in touch with you, Torrie. What happened? We swore we wouldn't drift apart. We never should have had that fight. . . .

Jay could tell I was thinking about her again. "Wanna go on the swings?" His voice cut through my silent wandering. I woke up.

Wake up, Torrie. All you have to do is show a sign that you're okay, I pleaded to myself.

"I'd love to. When you were little, did you ever have a contest to—"

"—see who could swing the highest?" we asked in unison. My laughter trailed off.

I wonder if you remember, Torrie. I always used to win. Well, not always. And now you're lying in a hospital, not knowing if you'll ever walk again.

I forced myself to smile and continue the conversation. The swing was higher off the ground than I remembered.

"I bet I can go higher than you," he said. I shook my head. Leave it to Jay to turn a childhood pastime into a challenge. I rhythmically pumped my swing, and my hair blew around my face as I sailed through the air. I looked over at Jay. Although he had the same sparkle in his eye and he threw me the same half-smile he always did, there was something different about him. Or maybe there was just something different about the way I saw him. The sparkle fell from his face.

"Oh, Liz, smile."

I really wanted to, but it hurt to smile. I couldn't tell if the wind was burning my face or if it was the single tear that rolled down my cheek.

We hopped off the swings and started to walk back toward his car.

"You know," he started, "you'll do so much better if you keep your mind busy with something else."

God, Torrie, why did you have to be so stupid? Why did you have to get in the car with someone who was drunk? You never even saw the curve in the road. The last thing you saw was the tree. . . .

"I'm sorry. What did you say?"

"Liz, let's talk. You want to know what ticks me off?"

"What?"

He almost didn't wait for my response.

"How the most beautiful girls hurt themselves for no reason."

I finally broke down, my blank stare welling up with tears.

"Come here."

I fell onto his shoulder. We stood there while he held me and let me cry. I finally realized what was so different about Jay: The sparkle in his eye was a tear I had never seen before.

"I want to fix the world so you never have to cry again," he said.

That night I cried for Torrie, and Jay cried for me. ▣

Maybe Tomorrow

by Kelly J. Van Deusen

I hate hospitals; they are cold and uninviting. My father is sitting next to me, carrying on a conversation with my mother that I cannot follow. I look back to my book. My mom is playing with a spoon left from her dinner. She smiles as she talks, but it's not really her. She is weak and vulnerable sitting there in front of me. I try to smile, but I do not recognize her. She looks the same, but here she is no longer that strong and fearless woman. On our way to her room, we bought her a stuffed brown dog that she now clutches playfully. I force a grin.

I don't know how I should feel. I don't really like to deal with illness or death. It's something that should never affect me. I know she will be all right, but I hate the fact that she is sick at all. I hate her for being sick, but I don't *really* hate her. I love her. I push the negative thoughts to the back of my mind. My mother starts to talk to me. Taking this opportunity, my father leaves. I sit uncomfortably alone with her. She smiles, as though she is signaling me to say something.

I try not to notice. I don't know what to say. There is a barrier of stubbornness and strength between us. She didn't tell me she was sick; she was trying to protect me.

I didn't tell her I was worried; I didn't want to scare her. She'll be all right.

Outside in the hall, the nurses are talking about the elections. "You won't be able to vote tomorrow," I say. She nods. The conversation ends. I try desperately to think of something good to say. There are a thousand things I *should* say, that I want to say, but for some reason I don't know how.

I hate seeing her sick. She tells me to be good, to drive safely, to make her Jell-O and take care of Daddy. I nod. Silence. I mention briefly my school day, the quiz I took and what I had for lunch—things that aren't really relevant to this present situation. I want to tell her I love her, that she is the world to me, that I am sorry for the fights we've had, but the words are trapped behind our barrier. My father comes in; it is eight o'clock and visiting hours are over.

She smiles. My father bends over and kisses her. It is their first night apart since they've been married. She plays with the stuffed dog and laughs like a child. I kiss her good night. She reminds me to make her Jell-O; I smile. I feel tears swelling inside of me. *She is so vulnerable,* I think, and she needs me so much right now, but I am too afraid. I will see her tomorrow. She will be okay. The preliminary tests look good.

We stand at the door, wave good-bye and then head down the hallway. The tears run down my cheeks. I scold myself; I need to be strong. I want to turn back and tell her how important she is to me, but the nurses are already in the room checking her. I hate myself at this moment. She needs me, and I have let her down. I have missed another chance to tell my mother what she means to me. Maybe tomorrow I will tell her. I turn my head so my tears aren't visible to my father.

On the drive home, we talk about who will win the election. The conversation is annoying because all I can think about is what I should have said to my mother. When we arrive home, I sense something is not right. She will be home soon, maybe even tomorrow. I go to the kitchen and boil the water for her Jell-O. ◙

Photo by Amanda J. Luzar

I Wish

by Mary-Helena McInerney

What?
Did you say something?
　　　Sorry.
I thought you did.
　　　Or,
Maybe it's that
　　　I wish
You did.

During those awkward
Moments of silence,
On the phone,
Late at night.

I wish
　　　You
Would have asked me many
Different things
　　　Like . . .

Did you see
So and so
Get in trouble
During lunch?

Or,
Do you
Understand
The Chemistry
work?
'Cause I don't.

What about,
Do we have
A short day
Tomorrow?
I heard the teachers
had a meeting.

Simple
  Things.
Like
That.
Would have
Made my day.

Just because,
  I was
Talking
  To
    You.

Almost a Sister

by Stephanie Hook

The day began like any other that year, my mom waking me in the dark morning with a soft, "Stephanie, wake up." But this morning I could tell by her voice that something was wrong. Right away I knew what it was that would fill my eyes with tears, and so I wrapped my arms around her. Then she said it, putting all doubt to rest. "She's gone. She's with the angels now." At first, of course, it was a shock, even though Kristen had been battling cancer for two long years. I didn't want to believe it, but I knew I had to face the truth. For her, the suffering was over, but for everyone else the pain had just begun.

The long, hot shower helped me collect my thoughts. A number of things ran through my mind: *What do you say to your best friend of so long when she has lost her only sibling? How can God take away such a great friend, sister and confidante?* The thought of the rest of my life without Kristen scared me so much that I didn't know what to say. Having the mental image of Kristen with wings kept a smile in me. I didn't know it then, but that image would keep me going—bringing a smile to my face to this day.

Although the ride to Jenna's house takes only eight minutes, it seemed like forever this morning. I couldn't stop my tears. They just came and came. As the trees outside went rushing by in slow motion, my mom leaned over and said, "I know it's hard, but we have to be strong. We have to be tough for Jenna, Elaine and even for Doug." She was right. I had to try my hardest to dry my tears before we reached their house.

As we pulled into that familiar driveway, the big house never looked so lonely. The sun was just creeping in the sunroom door. There were two figures standing in the kitchen, Miss Elaine and Mr. Dougie—my second parents. They had played a huge role in raising me since Jenna and I were pretty much inseparable. We embraced with big hugs, and the tears flowed. In the background, I could hear the familiar voice of the woman I called Aunt Lorie. She wasn't my aunt, but she might as well have been. She was on the phone trying to maintain a calm voice. She was the bearer of bad news.

I was glad to see them, but I had to find Jenna.

I crept up the stairs and peeked around the corner. There she was asleep in the comfy waterbed, snuggled with her ratty old Pooh Bear. I didn't want to wake her, so I just crawled in next to her and dozed off. I woke up two hours later to the sound of Jenna's stirring. Her face lit up when she saw me. "Stepho," she yelled and threw her arms around me. "That's just like you, always here when I need you!" I think just being together made us both feel a bit more secure.

Wednesday, November 19 was one of the longest days of my life. The whole house was in a whirlwind. Men were in and out to take Kristen's medical supplies. Friends and family gathered to chat quietly, offer their condolences, and even to laugh about the fun memories we all had of Kristen. Jenna and I simultaneously burst out into our rendition of Billy Joel's "In the Middle of the Night." Jenna, Kristen and I made up our version years earlier on one of our Girl Scout trips. We could never go a week without singing it and having our bellies hurt from laughing so hard. It made me think, especially about how close I really was to Kristen. She was always there, like a big sister, helping with guy situations, offering advice. Since she was only two years older, she and I had many of the same problems in addition to her battling cancer and trying to lead a normal life. She was awesome, an all-around great person, and now she was gone, just like that.

It was totally weird. I was sad because I had lost someone so great, but at the same time I was happy knowing that she was no longer in pain. She was where she could have eternal bliss, and eternal bliss is what Kristen deserved. She touched my life in a way no one else ever will, a way I cannot describe with words. It's a feeling that I don't often find, but Jenna, Elaine, Doug and I, and everyone who knew Kristen, felt it.

We are forever lucky to have known her, to have been cared for by Kristen. She wasn't a selfish person. In fact, she left one of her possessions for each of us. I'll forever cherish her sweet little purse that I had always adored, the bucket hat that we picked out together on a trip and one of her favorite stuffed dolphins. Whenever I touch them, I can feel the warmth and love of Kristen. I know she wanted it that way, too.

Because Kristen was involved in many activities, the whole town missed her. She played sports, everything from cheerleading to basketball. She did many extra-curricular activities. She helped out at the local food and clothing bank, and was the vice president of the middle school. And one of her biggest loves was being a member on the children's board at the University of Georgia Children's Hospital.

She had so much going for her, and it was all taken away. Her first diagnosis was in seventh grade when she was treated for bone cancer of her knee. After that, she went into remission. She threw a big party, which was a blast. We all were convinced she had beat it!

But a few weeks later, she relapsed. They found cancer in her lungs. It had spread, and there was no stopping it. She was slipping into God's hands. We had to get used to the idea that Kristen was dying and we couldn't save her.

During her last few months, she accomplished some amazing things. She modeled and had her story published in a national teen magazine. She had the chance to swim with her favorite animal, the dolphin, and to travel to the Mall of America, the much-loved Disney World, and Los Angeles to meet the cast of *Party of Five*. Kristen felt as though she completed her life and never complained about having cancer. She had incredible strength to get through it while keeping a smile on her face. Kristen has definitely been an inspiration to those she met. She is now my guardian angel, and I know she watches over me, protects me and helps me do the right thing. I love her. I don't mourn her death; I celebrate her life. ▣

Somewhere

by Cecilia Woodworth

Somewhere
In the sticky heat and warm afternoon rains,
With chigger-bite-covered legs
That made me look like a beaten child,
Wearing a tight, green skirt with a loose, white shirt and
Bright orange flip-flops,
And skin with no makeup,
But covered in a film of sweat, suntan lotion and DEET,
I learned I was beautiful
And maybe someone nice would love me again
And that I was ready for them.

Somewhere
In a house filled with strangers who were really my
*   closest friends,*
With Diet Coke and rum-filled glasses that weren't
*   allowed,*
But tasted sweet and warm
Drunk outside with dirty, bare feet and endless giggles,
Before a conversation that started out right,
But ended in tears and a hug
That told me everything I already knew and denied for
*   too long,*

I learned that my problems would only grow until I
faced them
And opened my heart to unsaid apologies.

Somewhere
In a strange place filled with strange people who spoke a
strange tongue,
Pretending to work and flirting during water breaks
With rowdy boys who stopped and stared
At my pale skin and yelled things I couldn't understand,
But still answered with a smile and hola,
And listening to bad techno on an old bus,
With a future yuppie trying to hold my hand,
Assuming that beers at eight in the morning impressed
me,
Feeling my heart ache while looking at an old picture
Before bed in the spare room,
I learned that I could stop needing him and being sad,
And I could survive without a boyfriend.

Somewhere
In the drizzling rain and mud that sucked at my boots,
In scrubs that weren't mine and a Mt. Rushmore shirt
With the sleeves tucked under my bra straps,
With everything aching from my shoulders to my back,
Drinking warm water and too much Coke
While throwing chicken bones to starving dogs,
After hauling blocks in the ninety-degree sun
With gloves a size too big and oil on the tip of my long
braid,
I learned I was stronger than I ever thought,
And good for more than just getting A's.

Somewhere
In a week that was too short but just long enough to
   change everything,
With eleven new mothers
Who talked about me when they thought I couldn't hear,
Braided my hair, said no to late-night discos,
Carried my stuff when I got tired,
And shared their seat towel and shirttail,
With three new fathers
Who rubbed my shoulders and bought me ice cream,
With three new older brothers
Who teased, pulled my hair with a smile and stole my
   bandanna,
And with two new sisters
Who shared their stories about love, sex and drugs
And laughed about nothing for hours on a bunk bed,
The whole time worrying about breaking it with their
   weight,
I learned that family doesn't have to share genes,
Only love, which comes more quickly than I ever
   thought,
And can bring peace to my entire life.

Somewhere
Between leaving on a fall afternoon with a feeling of
   dread and nervousness
And coming home to an empty house with a full heart
   and too much dirty laundry,
Feeling insecure and wondering if I brought too
   many shoes
And not enough personality,

But being the ultimate to cover my fears while
Hooking anyone up with anything,
And shakin' my groove thing to loud Spanish music
*   in a scary, old van*
That Myrtle fell out of and I held her hand,
Wanting to be as brave and tough as she,
I learned I was a good person and people should
*   like me,*
Because I am something special.

The week of hot days and long nights with noisy
*   air conditioners*
I spent in a place that's dirty and poor called Honduras,
I did more than help people who just have bad luck,
I helped me learn how to be me,
And like it.

Peter Rabbit Wore Wool

by Jana Richardson

He was never my favorite grandfather. It hurts to admit that. His house was big and dark and always cold. My grandmother smoked, and we always went home smelly. I did love him. I loved him a lot. My head was always buried in his wool sweaters when he hugged me. Whenever I picture him, I see him in them. I think he wore them when he golfed. Grammy gave me some when he died. They're warm.

At holidays he was such a presence. When he laughed, you heard him. When he yelled, your eyes watered. He had a lisp when he talked; maybe it was a bit of an accent, I don't know. My cousins and I loved to play board games with him. He was the only adult who would play with us. He never let us win as some grown-ups do. In fact, he usually blew us out of the water.

Our favorite was the Peter Rabbit game. We haven't played it in years. It had tiny metal pieces painted in pastel colors. Grandpa was always Peter. Kathy liked to be the frog or the hen. I was usually the pink "girl" bunny. It had tiny little dice to roll and a beautifully drawn playing board. When the game was over, we always begged to play again. We never did. Once was enough for him.

My grandpa had a heart attack. It was his second. He

died in the morning. They didn't tell us. I spent that Monday at school just like everyone else.

My mom said there wouldn't have been any point in crying and moping. That was the point.

I felt guilty.

We had an open casket viewing for the family. He was just asleep in the wooden box. I don't think I'd ever seen him sleep. It was strange to see my dad cry. It was strange to hear that music. It was strange. My dad asked if I wanted to touch him. I didn't want to. I barely touched him in life, except for those wool hugs.

I touched his cheek. It was hard. It was cold. It wasn't the old, squishy cheek I used to kiss. That made me feel a little better. Maybe this wasn't my grandfather.

The last time I saw him was at my dance recital. I came into the audience during the performance to say hi. They left at intermission because his chest hurt. I asked Grandma at the funeral if I had hugged him. She said I did. I was glad. Now I remember. He was wearing wool. ▣

Seeds We Sow

by B. J. Simmons

We've got to grow our home
From the seeds we sow
We feed the walls
With screams of anger
We flush the happiness
While inflicting so much pain
And waste hours upon hours
In front of the television
He tells us "it's okay"
He tells us "it's normal"
"All families fight and
All families hate
All families will destroy the rest of your life"
We go to the fridge
To chill our hearts
And to dull our senses
For the next massacre
But when we go out
We never forget our masks
To hide the distraught faces
We have molded ourselves

Red Guilt

by Holly Hester

It was a warm, sticky evening, and I heard the rumble of a distant thunderstorm. I walked outside and looked up into the sky. Dark, threatening clouds were approaching at the edge of the horizon. A sudden gust of cold wind brought the smell of burning charcoal to my nostrils. I shivered in anticipation. Suddenly, my mother bellowed from the kitchen, "Holly, Susie, come and shuck this corn!" Irritated, I chose to ignore her and casually pretended to be deaf. Unfortunately, my younger sister emerged from the house with a bundle of corn in her arms just as I was planning my escape. Sensing my intention, my sister snapped at me to help with the corn. I stomped over to the bushel and grabbed an ear from her arms. I just happened to whack her over the head with it simultaneously. In a furious rage, my sister dropped them and rushed toward me, red faced, fists clenched and uttering words of unintelligible hatred. I expertly dodged her first advance (having years of sibling rivalry experience) and gave my sister a hard push in self-defense. Consequently, she tumbled to the ground face first.

At this point, I realized that I had probably exceeded my sister's limit of controllable rage, and began to worry about what act of violence she would be capable of. So, with a rapidly rising adrenaline level, I sprinted toward the house and swung open the back door. Not realizing my sister was just a few feet behind me, I slammed the door forcefully as I entered the house. Initially, I heard a paralyzing shatter of glass. In slow motion, I turned to see my sister's arm thrust through one of the glass panes. Almost instantly I heard high-pitched hysterical screams. I opened the door to see her wildly jumping up and down in pain. The glass had slashed her arm, creating a zigzag wound. I stood in shock as my mother instinctively grabbed a dish towel, placed it on the wound and rushed her to the hospital.

For several minutes, I stared at the splattered blood that covered our back door and white-tile hallway. I began to shake, crying with guilt. In an act of punishment, I forced myself to mop it up. As I scrubbed, tears fell and splashed into her blood. It was almost an eerie message of condemnation. The next morning, my sister came home with one hundred and thirty-two stitches in her arm. But, unlike her wound, mine will never heal. ▣

Sea of Green

by Katrina Lahner

The truck pulls up beside the rusty gate and screeches to a stop. She steps out onto the dirt road, outfitted in a pink dress three sizes too big. Her pigtails whip around her cheeks in the wind, the pigtails her daddy had done for her early that morning while he explained where they were going.

He comes around the truck now, flowers in hand, and picks her up. She rests her head on his shoulder. They pass through the gate into the green field. The contrast between the green grass and the gray stone slabs shocks her eyes. She is drawn to the flowers scattered across this sea of green. Last year, when they'd come, she'd asked if she could pick some of those pretty flowers, but her daddy said they belonged to someone else.

Their walk takes them almost to the back corner of this endless sea, to a spot where the sun has not yet given up hope of reaching. They arrive at their place, and her daddy sets her down. Holding her hand, he lays the flowers on the ground.

He squeezes her hand tightly and she squeezes right back. She knows he needs her here. She's not sure why, but she can tell that he is sad already. The silent tears have started their journey down his cheeks, wavering at the end of his nose and eyelashes as if afraid to fall.

He kneels down to hug her. She is used to these hugs from her daddy. Sometimes, when she is playing, she sees him watching her, as if remembering a dream. And she smiles at him, and he smiles back and reaches out to hug her.

He stands up now, taking tissues from his pocket. Facing the flowers, he says one last thing, casting his eyes to the ground. She stands respectfully, still holding his hand, while he finishes.

The green sea seems to have swallowed his truck, for she cannot see it from where she stands. The walk back is quiet, and she almost falls asleep in his arms.

As he buckles her into her seat, her mind wanders and she begins to dream. Her dreams are filled with an endless sea of green, dotted here and there with flowers. And amidst this vast ocean is her mother. ▣

Art by Grace Hyun Joo Chang

Neighbor Friend

by Valerie Bandura

What the moon saw
Was a brown-haired girl
Playing private eye on her lawn
With a flashlight beam
Catching off my window.

I gave her a haircut
That afternoon in her bathroom.
Standing on that cold tile floor
We compared feet sizes
As her hair fell like brown leaves
Around our ankles
Leaving our toes to jut out
Like rocks on the seafloor.

She said men's feet
Were too bent in general
And she covered her mouth and smiled
And said I could have been a statue
Holding down a great beast.
Like Davy Crockett.
And her conviction was ageless.
And her hands were silent

And I mistook her silence for strength
So that I could have promised her anything.

Now I sit on my floor
Watching the moon
Watch my neighbor on her lawn.
Her hair is much shorter now
And some ends hang off her head
Like a sharp catastrophe.

I couldn't help but send her off early
To catch up with me faster.

Photo by Carla English-Daly

Apple Pie

by Dina Cheryl Brandeis

Sunlight flooded my room, waking me. I heard the gentle howl of the wind outside my window. I knew it was cold, but under my covers I remained warm and cozy. I forced myself to get up; no lounging around in bed all day. As I kicked off my comforter, chills ran up and down my spine like a mild electric shock. I put on jeans, a sweater and a pair of thick socks.

I felt like rolling in the autumn leaves, climbing the tallest tree . . . or maybe going apple picking. The air was perfect for it: clean and fresh. I looked outside my window, two kids were playing football with their father next door. I heard the father yell, "Go long!" Maybe today was a day for playing football. No, not for me.

As I walked downstairs, I smelled fresh pancakes and syrup with sausages. My mom was wrapped in a terry-cloth robe, stacking the pancakes high on the plates. The sausages were on a white plate in the center of our wooden table. My dad was already positioned at the table anxiously waiting. I sat down, and my mom served the pancakes.

"So, what should we do today?" I looked outside the window.

My dad replied with a low bee-like hum, "How 'bout we go . . . apple picking?"

My head snapped toward my father and I thought, *Wow! Is that ironic?* I would not let it be known that I was a female copy of my dad (let's face it, I even look a little like him), so as I was about to answer him, the phone rang.

"Dad . . . Do you mind if I go over to Melissa's house because she's having this Halloween party, and she kind of, sort of, wanted me to help her get. . . ."

Before I could finish, my dad said, "Of course, we can go apple picking next weekend."

I felt bad, but I really wanted to go to Melissa's.

I got home about ten o'clock that night, but I had a plan. I woke my dad, who was asleep on the couch, and said, "Hey, Dad, wanna go apple picking?"

My dad's eyes lit up. "It's late."

"So?"

"I'll get my coat."

Dad and I went apple picking until one in the morning. When we got home, my stomach hurt from laughing all night. I fell right into bed, and when I awoke the next morning, I smelled fresh apple pie baking. ▣

I Had a Bad Time

Fiction by Alice Kinerk

I'm looking at the floor as five girls talk loudly around me, looking at each other. I sneak a look at a pair of sneakers lying forgotten beside my leg. I slide my eyes to the right like a detective. I don't turn my head, though; I don't want to attract attention. When you can't look anyone in the eye, you assume everyone else can, and you feel out of place. It is a shock when you realize a whole lot of people spend a whole lot of time talking to one another while looking away.

But I'm not listening to their conversations, although I do hear them and some of their excited energy seeps through the air into me. I'm twisting the rough fibers of the red shag rug around the first knuckle of my fingers, twisting it tight until the tips of my fingers are light pink berries that complement the screaming red of the rug. My back is curved in a comfortable C shape; I'm sitting cross-legged resting my chin on my hands. My long brown hair hides the sides of my face.

The house is dirty. There are small hills of clothes and toys and magazines on the floor. There is a sweater hiding a small radio in this bedroom, and only one dingy flat sheet lying twisted on the bed. The windows are covered with a strange, fine yellow dust, with patterns and pictures traced by children's fingers. The low ceiling is spotted with watermarks. There is an odd smell in the air, at times pleasant, like fabric softener, and at times pervaded with the much more intense smells of children and poverty. The kids I have seen—and there are several who quickly become indistinguishable in my mind—are quiet and wide-eyed. They follow me from room to room in an eerily silent pack, sucking on bits of blankets, fingers or hair. I smile at them and pick them up, but they wrestle free with surprising strength. Still, they stay silent.

The girls, however, can't seem to stop chattering. I'm listening not to what they are saying, but to how they are saying it. Each girl seems to be having her own conversation with the others in the room, throwing out an endless stream of words and giggles and quick pauses for breath or maybe thought. Every girl goes on, and no one seems to be listening to the garble of voices, except maybe me.

But their words aren't intended for me. I can't understand why Debby, whom I don't really know, invited me to her party, or why she wanted me here at all. I feel awkward and homesick, and in the same detective way, I search for a clock with my eyes. *If I could only know what time it is,* I think, *I could count the hours until I'm going home.* If I have something concrete to count and think about, time goes by faster. Right now, the girls are ignoring me, and that leaves me sitting here silently, burning with a sort of sad anger and resentment toward them for being able to socialize and speak so easily.

In a few minutes the air in the room is thick with the

smell of hair spray, the aerosol kind. Someone opens a window. I turn my face toward it and the low sun scars blue streaks across my vision that hover, ghostlike, against the black back of my eyelids when I shut them.

It is when I have my eyes shut that Debby finally turns around in the plastic chair to ask me if I'm having a fun time.

"Yeah," I say, my voice quiet and my tone too high. My throat is dry so I swallow hard and smile what I think must look like a genuine grin. Debby studies me for a moment.

"She hates it here." She pauses and glances back to me as if I will confirm it. "She either hates it here or she hates us. One or the other."

I open my eyes wide like I've seen the other girls do and shake my head from side to side violently, my hair sweeping back and forth across my face.

"No," I lie, laughing. "I'm having fun, but you guys are all talking about people I don't know, so I can't really join in."

Debby straightens her lips into a thin line and looks away from me at another girl. I look around from face to face and they all seem to be looking back at me expectantly, as if they have just asked me a question that I haven't answered. My tongue feels thick and immobile; I know there is no way I will be able to say another word. I begin twisting the rug again and sit tense until the feeling of five pairs of eyes on me fades away. ▣

A Glance in the Mirror

by Kelley Pastyrnak

I was playing with my baby doll in my room after dinner when the house grew very quiet. All I could hear was the hum of the dishwasher. I could smell the lemon soap my mother had just used to wash the kitchen table and the dusty scent from the vacuum cleaner my father had just run over the rugs.

The house was very still and dim. I could hear the water running as my father took a shower, and the television downstairs entertaining my brothers and sisters.

The scent of my mother's perfume filled my bedroom. I tiptoed across the dark hall, afraid of disturbing the unusual silence. The door to my parents' bedroom was open an inch, and I peered in. I saw my mother, dressed in a white blouse and black dress pants, putting on a gold necklace with a matching bracelet and earrings. She turned her head suddenly; she had spotted me. She motioned for me to come and sit on her bed as she continued to get ready. I lay on my stomach, my chin nestled in my hands as I looked at her in the mirror. Her gold jewelry reflected in the mirror, glistening brightly. Jet-black hair brushed the back of her neck. Her pretty, round face was so fair it almost matched the white of her freshly ironed blouse.

Again she squirted perfume on the soft insides of her wrists and rubbed them together. Lying on my mother's bed, looking at her in the mirror, I couldn't help but notice her exquisite beauty. She sat on the bed and put me on her lap.

"Emily will be here in a few minutes to watch you tonight," she said softly. "Your father and I are meeting some friends for dinner. We'll be back around nine." She hugged me and told me to go out and wait for Emily. As she hugged me, her scent grew stronger, and so did our love. 回

Omar, Are You Sleeping?

by Sofiya Cabalquinto

The morning I turned seven
my mother woke me earlier than usual
and led me, crusty-eyed, to the living room
where in a box lay a new Siamese.

And since that day I haven't
ever slept alone; beside me he lies all curled up,
head tucked against his belly
like any other cat would

Except that his eyes are always half open
the whites gleaming like pearl buttons through the slits.
And for that my father calls him Liberace
after the piano great who had one too many face-lifts.

Out of Focus:

Facing Challenges

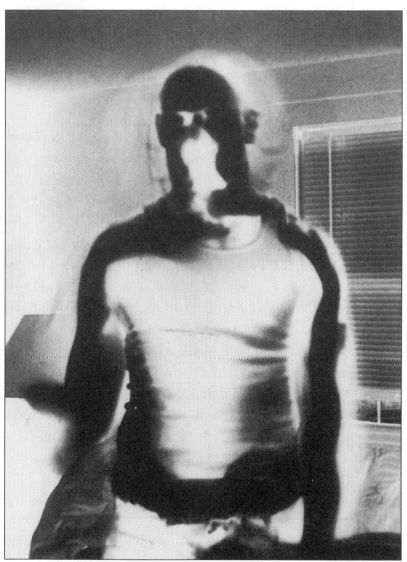

Photo by Peter Kelly Muller

The Black Bandanna

by Joe Capolupo

It was a typical Monday morning. I grabbed my books, kissed my mother good-bye and walked out the front door. As I ventured past a freshly painted, jet-black Caddy, I stopped to take a look at my reflection. Staring back was a fourteen-year-old thug with a shaved head wearing filthy cut-off jeans tattered around the bottom and paratrooper boots, white laces all the way up. I smiled, removed a black bandanna from my belt and tied it around my forehead. From there I walked to a friend's house two blocks down. I was nervous because I knew that later in the day I was going to have to fight three of my fellow gang members. I had missed two meetings, and that was the rule.

I made my way to Josh's place. It was small and dirty. The smell of dog waste lurked among the garbage left behind by months of constant drinking and belligerent partying. I walked around back, jumped through the bedroom window and ended Josh's slumber by blowing a bong hit in his face.

In the midst of our morning session, a neighbor came popping through the half-broken window. We said our hellos and exchanged gang signs. Our words, "White pride" and "Down white criminals," could be heard in the next room by Josh's mother, but she remained a recluse, too inebriated to face reality. She just lay in bed, half-crippled and eating tranquilizers like candy. Periodically, she would threaten to call the police.

Within twenty minutes we made it to the store and back: Two twelve-packs and a half ounce of weed between the three of us would be sufficient until afternoon. We were merrily intoxicated and blowing the beer bong horns by 9:00 A.M. It was time for morning entertainment.

We filled our beer bottles with gasoline, threw them into a burning trash can and ran like hell into the small backyard shed. From there we had the best view of the flames bursting into the air as a rich black mushroom cloud ascended, infecting the calm blue of the sky.

As they usually did, the explosions woke a neighbor. He took advantage of the noise and began firing his Tech-9 and .38-caliber handgun into the ground on our side of the fence.

We closed the morning hours with some weight lifting and more beer drinking. It was the perfect remedy for the alcohol poisoning I had accumulated over the weekend.

Noontime came, and we decided to venture to a friend's house. A short walk over the dirt and crabgrass and we were at Big Ed's front door. Ed was the twenty-six-year-old president of a local motorcycle gang. He weighed about 270 and stood six and a half feet. If his size wasn't intimidating, his cold green eyes were powerful enough to pierce a man's chest and rip the breath from his lungs. It was Ed's idea to start our gang.

We were greeted with the tastiest of marijuana and the finest of liquors. We sat, took out the peace pipe and began discussing what the day would bring. Ed was always calculating new schemes for us to make some cash. Stealing from construction sites and homes, lifting car stereos and ripping off registration tags were all quick and easy ways.

Ed had just begun describing his new idea when Josh's brother, Bear, came storming in. His face red and dripping with sweat; the enraged giant was too winded to speak a word. When he was able, Bear explained that his aunt had been beaten by her boyfriend. Josh sprang to the telephone to call other members.

I went to another room to call my parents. I told my mother I had just returned from school and was going to the park with friends. Instead of giving me permission, she told me to come home immediately. My grandmother had just returned from the hospital, and she needed me to look after her.

The other "brothers" quickly arrived. Six, including me, were chosen to go down and take care of the aunt's boyfriend. I took Josh and Bear aside and explained that I would always be there for them, but I had to look after my grandmother. I splashed some cold water on my face in a vain attempt to sober up. We exchanged gang signs, and I was off. The guys jumped into the bed of the gray, beat-up Chevy and drove off in a frenzy of drunken hatred; I was disappointed I couldn't go.

I went to my grandmother's house and returned to mine the following day. The ride home lasted an hour that seemed a lifetime. I was incredibly anxious to find out what had happened. As soon my car pulled into the driveway, I charged into the house and phoned Josh, but no one was there. I threw my clothes into the bedroom and ran down to the 'hood, but the block was like a ghost town. I could sense something was not right.

As I left, I noticed Bear's girlfriend pulling up to her house. I dashed over to learn any news, but before I got out a word, she said angrily, "Arrested!" A single tear dripped from her cheek and fell to the sidewalk. I could see the disgust on her face as she turned away. I was in shock.

Then the realization set in. Eric, a friend who was involved, came rushing toward me. Confirming my horror, he explained what had happened and how he managed to avoid the police. He then warned me that the cops would most likely be back to search the house for weapons and stolen items. Ed had instructed us to take everything illegal from Josh's house and stash it. In one truckload, we transferred everything to a nearby friend's house. With Josh's mother unaware, Eric and I decided to spend the night in our recently incarcerated friend's shed. It was a safe distance from the house, so we wouldn't be heard. A bottle of Jack Daniels and some high-powered LSD would comfort us through the evening.

During that entire night my thoughts were consumed with questions. How did just having fun turn into this? Why was I lucky enough to have escaped the fate of my friends? Would I be this lucky next time?

That night I realized my life was being wasted. The only things I put effort into were getting high and proving to people how tough I was, how much intoxication I could withstand, and just how far I would go to show it. I needed out.

I woke up the next morning to a series of explosions. When I looked, there were no friends with bottles of gasoline. The ATF [Bureau of Alcohol, Tobacco and Firearms] had thrown percussion grenades into the neighboring houses. From that small, filth-encrusted window, I watched black uniformed agents with submachine guns blaring swarm the surrounding backyards. They began hurling the men, women and children to the cold, wet grass. More blasts, followed by high-pitched screams, could only mean the raid had spread farther down the street.

In the midst of the insanity, my attention suddenly turned to Ed kneeling in the mud, his hands restrained behind his back. Everything else hushed. My focus was fixed on the man who, to us, had always signified power, respect and courage. I watched his screams of anger turn to tears of horror as he watched his wife and four-year-old son taken into custody. His scowling face was like an open book. I could read his fear as the agents ran in and out of the house, each time seizing guns, drug paraphernalia and stolen goods. From the shed window, that life didn't seem so wonderful anymore.

Right then and there, I vowed that if I made it out of there, everything would be different. I was ready for things to change. I had seen enough to know I didn't want it anymore.

Afraid to use the bathroom or even open the door for air, I hid on a mattress inside that hovel for five hours.

Eric tried to escape, but was caught as soon as he left the backyard.

The air had grown silent. It seemed that the lunacy had ended. I gazed outside to see the path of devastation that lingered behind the morning's chaos. The personal belongings of the people I cared about were scattered like ashes on the floor of a burning forest. I left the neighborhood and the cloud that had long been shadowing me with a false perception of life and what was important. I didn't understand why I had been so lucky, but I knew I was being handed the opportunity to regain the life I had so quickly forgotten.

As I approached my house, I lowered the black bandanna from my brow and grasped it in my fist. I walked to the backyard and sat in front of a half-broken cinderblock where I laid the emblem I had worn so proudly, the symbol that once represented a brotherhood of courage and pride. My eyes closed, and a moment of serenity came over me. I felt the warmth of the fire rise to my face as I inhaled the smoke of my seemingly impenetrable bonds and exhaled the breath of a new life. It was over. I had just begun. ▣

A Quiet Enemy

by Beth Victoria Adair

Her arms were thin and pale. Her complexion was sallow and she had dark circles under her eyes. Shadows filled the voids in her indented cheeks. She smiled weakly. I tried to keep from crying, but salty tears began to fall. I wrapped my arms around her. Her body was so thin; she smelled stale and was very cold. I held her bony elbow as I helped her up the stairs to my room.

Years of photographed memories hung on my wall. The days when we played dress-up and world-famous models were gone. This wasn't a game anymore; my best friend was dying. We sat on the floor and faced each other. She asked for a blanket because she was cold; she was always cold. I asked if she could finally accept that she was anorexic; she nodded and looked down. My mind raced; I did not know what to say. I told her I did not know much about anorexia, but I loved her and would do anything I could to help. She said what I needed to do was be there for her.

For the rest of the day we talked, but I realized I could not cure her; it was up to her. I learned that her diet was pinto beans and lettuce. People would stare at her at school and whisper when she walked by.

Then one night, when my parents were out at a meeting, my brother and I sat at home watching television when the phone rang.

"Hello."

"Beth, it's me." She was crying.

"What's wrong?"

"I'm at the hospital. The doctor said I would have died if I had not come. They don't know if I will make it until Christmas. Beth, I need you," she choked through the sobs.

She was in the eating-disorder unit. Ironically, it was right next to the maternity ward. Every day when I went to visit her, I walked by crying babies and happy mothers. Then I would walk into her unit. Thin, pale bodies wandered aimlessly, not knowing whether they wanted to live or die; all they knew was that they felt horribly overweight. I did all I could to try to cheer her up. I brought teen magazines but found that all they emphasized were issues of weight and body image. I brought pictures of us together when we were younger, but took them back when she made comments about how fat she was then. I could not believe this: Where had my best friend gone? My talkative, loud, brave, wild friend was shy, depressed, angry and waiting to die. One time when I was in her room, we walked by the mirror. She looked at her reflection.

"God, look at me. I look horrible."

I looked at her. "Yes, you do."

With that, she laid her head on my shoulder and cried. Every night I prayed that she would gain weight and go home, but it took months. Even when she did come home, things were not great. She exercised every day and ate only certain things, always watching her diet. She was still quiet and shy, reserved and depressed, nothing like she had been. Every day I wished this had never happened, that I was still the timid one and she was the outgoing one who would always push me to let my feelings out.

But I am thankful. Thankful that she survived, thankful I still have her as a friend. ▣

Photo by Patrick Michael Baird

She Tried

by Dana C. Silano

She tried to tell me that she was no junkie
  As we stood talking over coffee and cigarettes
She pouted her best CK pout
  And covered the inside of her elbow
  Declaring simply and doubtfully:
  "I'm no junkie."

I stared down at my imperfect thighs
  And compared them to her purple veiny legs

I had to smile.

She tried to tell me that she was no junkie
  As she popped three mini-thins
  And politely offered them to me
She gulped them down with coffee,
  And took a drag from her cigarette
  Declaring simply and dishonestly:
"I'm no junkie."

Another Step Closer

by Janelle Adsit

He hid in his crumpled sheets, his pillow wet. He turned his head to the ceiling above. His body clenched stiffly. The room was drowned in his silence. He breathed rhythmically; that was all the effort he could manage. His intense green eyes glazed over. I crept in through the door.

My eyes peeked at his, drooping and forming tiny slits. His eyes peeled open. His body started to tremble. He bolted upward like a bullet released from its chamber. His eyes gleamed. He'd spotted me. I took a step toward him. I pressed a smile on my face. He swung his bare feet over the side of the bed. He put them on the brown carpet. He lifted his body slowly from the edge of the bed, like an old man arising from his nap. He took a threatening step toward me. His face shriveled, decorated with deep trenches. He reached up and slapped both his hands on the sides of my face. He yanked my face closer to his. His piercing eyes stared straight at me. His lips started to move and with them came an earth-shattering sound. He shook my head. His hollering intensified. He squeezed the sides of my head.

He took a step closer. I stepped back. Another step closer; another step back. I was slammed against the wall. His bellows did not cease. He continued to jerk my head, slamming it into the wall behind him. His eyelids gritted together, forming tiny half-moons.

My eyes stretched, trying to strip the glaze shadowing them. I reached up with both hands. My fingers ripped his hands from my face. I slipped under his blocking arm. He pivoted. His arm still hung suspended. Suddenly, silence fell over him. A sly smile crawled onto his face. I stared back at him. He took a step toward me. I lifted my left foot. I pivoted. With my back facing him, I strode out of the room. I never glanced back. ▣

Art by Justin W. Avery

Watching Her

by Holly Eddy

She's bent over her garden,
tending to weeds that insist on bingeing on
her soil.
I see her touch her back
and I know she's in pain,
but won't admit it.
Taking a deep breath,
she stands up and turns around.
Startled to see me standing there
watching her,
she laughs a little.
I point to the sky and
ask her to come in,
"A few minutes," she replies.
I walk back into the house
and watch her gather flowers;
the clouds roll in,
and I see her look at the sky
and smile as if the gods have
sent her the rain.
It is then that I realize what I'll
miss the most when I'm gone:
Mother stooping to point out
the finer things in life.

The Journal

by Joelle M. Shabat

My memories of my mother are quite different from most children's. Most maternal figures are usually viewed as the epitome of strength, reliability and protection from any evils that approach their children; they seem to possess magic that radiates in times of distress. These occasions are few and far between for me. Most of my memories are of her crying hysterically in the shower next to my room as her hair fell out; sitting in chemotherapy rocking mindlessly with tubes and needles coming from her arm like a heroin addict; lying prone on a couch, a gaunt skeleton resembling a victim of Auschwitz, the faded shadow of the full-figured woman she once was; her moaning from pain, tormented even while she slept. I still sleep with my stuffed bear over my head to ward off any noise that remotely resembles something that heart-wrenching.

My mother died on May 26, 1997, at 9:55 A.M. in a hospice wing, which was the most sterile, cold place one could spend their last moments. I arrived five minutes too late. Even though she had been in a coma, it would have made all the difference for me to see her alive one last time.

That night, I read the seventeen-page journal that she

had written for me. Nothing ever impacted me as much as those pages. As I sat on the couch and read, my father read over my shoulder and once again commenced his pathetic rendition of crocodile tears. As I watched him, I found myself completely devoid of sympathy for his alleged loss; all had been lost to him years ago, not today, and certainly not now. Then, he had been an untouchable icon placed upon a pedestal of infallibility, but had systematically knocked himself off through broken promises and transparent lies. I had been young and had known no better than to believe all he said as though it were the gospel, learning the truth of his words too late.

And now here he was, hovering over my shoulder as though he had every right to be there, to read my mother's personal thoughts, as though he were actually a part of our family. I didn't feel that he belonged here at all. It was during the next few months that I learned to hate him as my mother had for all he had done to her and to us. I don't know if I will ever wholly forgive him.

Her funeral was the next day. I spoke in front of that blurred, faceless crowd. All I remember is standing next to her plain poplar casket. The memories that I carry with me are like photographs; I can recount single moments in a detailed way while long periods of time are clouded in my mind. I have come to realize that they did not just bury her that day; they buried a piece of my soul and left an irreplaceable void inside me. I was left with the task of rearranging the shattered remnants of my identity into some coherence.

Days without her swelled into years, and time carried

me up and down through my confused sea made salty with tears on my quest to reconfigure who I was. I poured my energy into anything that would consume the seemingly infinite time. This was my evolution, where I defined my character, intelligence versus wisdom, and love that are who I am today.

Living with guilt, especially about someone who has died, is unbearable since you cannot find that person and be absolved. In an attempt to purge myself, I began to take a good look at myself, analyzing my attitude and motivation for acting the way I did. I saw what I had done in selfishness, anger and bitterness as manifestations of emotions that I didn't know how to deal with, and a complete disregard for the will and needs of others. But I began to adhere to morals that centered around honesty and integrity.

Intelligence is a relative term. Always the straight-A student, I worked hard to achieve excellence and recognition. But the experience of my mother's death has taught me that academic intelligence, though valuable, is applicable only in a certain realm of life. Wisdom, however, is the most valuable form of intelligence and comes through life experience.

I have found that unconditional love is the rarest phenomenon. Most love people have for each other is conditional and ever-changing. Unconditional love is almost nonexistent, be it romantic or familial love. The only person who truly loved me unconditionally was my mother. She accepted me for who I was (even when I was probably the kid from hell) and loved me unquestioningly. There may never be a person with whom I am that comfortable. In the midst of all of the pain, there were beautiful, unforgettable moments.

My mother loved laughter and survived largely on humor. She often found the stupidest things funny and could make the most grotesque faces and noises. She had a sense of humor accompanied by a devilish girl's laugh that only those who had never completely grown up could revel in.

She adored her friendships and could talk for hours on the phone about absolutely nothing. Her closest friends would come and sit by her on the couch. Our cousin Debbie visited often, including me in these intimate moments when she sat between us and allowed her fingers to entwine separately the dark hair of mother and daughter.

Usually, an individual is affected the most by those who have been actively involved in his or her life. In my case, a mother's death was the commencement of the rebirth of her daughter. ▣

The Balcony

by Hannah R. Tadros

Oh, what a journey it's been—from there to here, from then to now. Must I go back? But something's calling me to return once more, a voice crying in the wilderness—the burdened voice of a spirit.

The endless, downward spinning finally stops. The air around me is harsh and oppressive—a heavy darkness on the surface of my mind and soul. I turn up the air conditioning and lie on the moist bed. Drip, drop, drip, drop; I stare at the distant, indifferent air-conditioning unit protruding from the wall above my head. I move my soggy pillow when I realize the tears it weeps are not clear but brown. Sighing, I sweep the room with my eyes. The massive mahogany wardrobe that should contain my clothes presses against the brownish-yellow wall; it totters and threatens to fall at the slightest provocation. I ignore it and wipe the sweat from my hands and face.

How do the beggars manage? Walking among the waste, sleeping with the strays, covered in layers of clothing—how do they do it? Don't they feel snared by the Egyptian sun's scorching fingers—nowhere to go— trapped? I scream in frustration and slap the air around me as my thoughts are interrupted by three infuriating flies. I shudder silently as I think of what else inhabits my room. Fleeing, I push the door and walk in on Mama and Chrissie. They jerk, and after an awkward moment, begin to laugh and joke. It's not the first time I've unexpectedly intruded on one of their hushed conversations. Yes, yes, protect the little one; she doesn't remember most of it. She doesn't need to know.

But don't worry. I'm prepared for this battle. I promise I am. I stare at Mama with a grin plastered on my face. She's been crying—not the kind of crying she does in front of me or even in front of Chrissie; these are unselfish tears—tears not for past pain, but for the future—tears of fear, tears for me. The doorbell sounds, shattering the deep silence of the house.

Bang! Bang!

It is the noise when fist meets face.

It is the sound of a wailing woman.

It is the noise of a breaking home.

It is the battle cry.

I pull and push at the door and finally get it open. The heat of the streets forces its way through the unguarded entrance into the house, into my brain, into my mouth. I stare down. I smile and laugh; I don't know why, because inside I cry. This will be a long one. I steady myself and prepare to do battle. "Hello, Daddy."

It's mid-battle. I'm wounded. I need to recover. Cursing myself for my weakness, I step onto the balcony. The air burdened with smoke and dirt is lighter out here. I steady myself against the burning metal railing and breathe. It is the air of dusk. The stench of garbage permeates the atmosphere. Looking down, I see the beggars

I once pitied, and I envy them. My eye catches the form of a stool in the terrace corner; I study it for a while. I bring it near the balcony edge, its crude, splintering skin grinding against the strength of the concrete wall. It's wounded also, its leg broken and scabbed. But it stands. It doesn't need four legs—three are enough. I laugh and again face the door. I am ready for battle; I am ready for war. And someday I will be ready for a truce. □

Photo by Shira Bergman

I Was Ten

by Tiffany A. Evans

All my life my father drank, so it was never anything out of the ordinary at my house. He would come home, have some beers, get buzzed and go to bed. Some days he would get carried away with the drinking and become rowdy. Those were the days that bothered me.

In school, we started studying alcohol abuse and the effects of drinking. At first, I didn't relate it to my father, but after a while I put two and two together. I began to realize that my father, my daddy, had a problem with this terrible substance.

My father's drinking was never talked about in our home. I think I was twelve when I finally asked my mother about it. She, of course, said he did not have a problem. Life continued just peachy keen, but really it was not.

My father's drinking kept getting worse. I wouldn't ask my friends to come over because I never knew what shape my father would be in. As I learned more about what alcohol actually did, I began to be afraid of him when he drank. Sometimes he acted totally different when he was drunk. I was so embarrassed by him. I knew it was not normal for him to drink so much; my friends' dads did not drink like he did. He was getting drunk every day, and he didn't act like himself anymore. My mom and I started to talk about his problem because it was tearing our family apart. We tried to get him help, but he would not admit he had a problem.

After rehab and many Alcoholics Anonymous meetings, my father was not much better, so my mother made the hardest decision of her life: She told him she wanted to separate until he was better. This was definitely not easy for my family. My dad moved out and my mom, my brother and I lived alone, without our daddy.

It was the greatest challenge I have ever faced. I had to learn that it was not my father who was bad, but the alcohol. I had to learn to forgive him for causing us so much pain, and realize that it was not his fault. I had begun to hate him, and I needed to learn to love him again. Eventually, I did, but I will never forget how much it hurt.

After three months of separation, my father was a totally changed man. He had a new job, new clothes, new everything. He completely changed his lifestyle. Most important, he had been sober the entire time.

My parents got back together. I was learning to forgive him, too. After a while we finally felt like a family again.

To this day, my father has not touched a drop of alcohol. He has been sober now for years. He promised us that he would never drink again as long as he lives, and I believe him.

And, just like my father, I know I will never drink either. ▣

Art by Emily Allen

Forgetting to Remember
by Adrienne Franceschi

The worst thing you can do is forget. We do not mean to; it just happens. When something devastating occurs, our mind's and body's focus is to survive. Often, what we mistake for courage is cowardice. By the second stage of grief—anger—we fight to keep our emotions down, to stop the sadness and hatred from rising through our throats into our brains. Sometimes that struggle becomes caught in our lungs and squeezes our breath until we gasp.

"Well, it's important to me. It's important to a lot of people." My mother's voice comes in uneven sobs as she struggles to speak her mind against the obstinate teenagers facing her—my sister and me.

"So what. We're the ones who have to go through everything again. We're the ones who get to be stared at in church, and it would be weird having all my friends there," my younger sister says in a half-angry, half-patronizing tone.

"Yeah. Who cares what other people think? Haven't we learned that we do things our way? We always have," I plead and complain, knowing I am putting my mom in an awkward position, backing her into a corner. Anger bubbles as I am forced to remember something I had finally learned to forget.

"It's customary to have a memorial Mass every five years. Nana has one every year. What is she going to think if we don't have one?"

This need to please my father's mother has always puzzled me. I don't like it. It makes everything seem fake and, what's worse, my sister and I are the only connection my mother has to my nana. In the old days we were one big family. It did not matter that my mother had only married into the family. Now we are the one reason she keeps in touch with them.

We sulk as Mom continues, "Do you want me just to forget? I'm not going to forget Gary." The expression on her face is impossible to look at as she bursts into tears and spits out the words, "I hope that when I'm dead you'll take the time to think about me once every five years."

She escapes into the bathroom and continues crying while I try not to take her words to heart. I have no urge to console her, no need to say I'm sorry and give in. I hate myself for that. I know I'm not being mature, but I can't help it. My heart wants to have a tantrum.

A day later, my mom tells me she will do as we asked and not have a memorial service for my father. This should be a victory, but really it's the opposite. By now I have cooled off and realize the logic of what she was saying. The thing is, it's just too late. The damage has already been done, and my damn pride won't allow me to believe otherwise. If I had only let myself remember and taken the time to grieve, then I would have pleased my mother. I would have had a good cry that I badly needed. It would have consoled my family. It would have been important to my father. It would have been respectful and shown the world I still love and miss my dad. Would have. ▣

A Blossom

by Steven Lam

Many gathered around your bed when
  You finally fell away.
I was there with them
Behind their circle of grief,
Hurdling through their silent sighs
While they threw their roses of affection.
And I?
  Have yet to toss my thoughts away
  Or drape my ribbon around a blossom
  To settle upon your bed.
  Nor have I given you a tender kiss
  Or wetted eye
To say a mournful good-bye.
And while they go on to pass you by,
I am here to sit with you and the grass
  in your lonesome hours
  Not the masses who have trickled
  Nor those who have dropped their
    Budding flowers in the midst of your angel cross.
And I, who have been to your bed
  When the wind chased the leaves,
  On a midnight run,

Through a summer's course
And a spring's malignant temper
Come not with an army of bouquets or ribbons.
But with a smile and intimate conversation
Come not with sorrow and regret,
But for an unforgivable stubbornness to keep
a friend alive.

You Alone

by Sarah E. Allen

As my sister tossed her chestnut curls over her shoulders, the sun gently shone its approval with a soft glowing light. I wanted to throw up. For my twelve years, Christine had been my best friend, my confidante, my role model and, most important, my big sister. Until recently, when two very influential feelings entered my life: inadequacy and jealousy.

Christine is the sister everyone wants to have but almost nobody does. It is commonplace when my friends call to talk to her for five minutes before asking for me. How many times have adults and friends commented that my sister is beautiful, talented and kind? Because of my struggle to accept these remarks, I taught myself that I must laugh politely and let their input be just another lovely nugget of wisdom to store away in a place that prevents my heart from breaking.

When, on the rare day I feel pseudo self-confident and content, Christine would emerge from her room like an exquisite butterfly from a cocoon, and my hopes of being "the pretty sister" for the day would be smashed. Perhaps the worst blow came in seventh grade, when I discovered that the boy I really liked had similar feelings—only for her. My resentment became a mixed jumble of admiration and depression, and I began a frantic search for a way out of this net of insecurity. Although this portrait may sound dark and frightening, perhaps the most haunting part was this: Christine had no idea of her power, nor would she ever dream of willfully inflicting such feelings on me. I was the only one to blame.

One evening, these tumultuous emotions reached their breaking point: Christine had a date to the school dance, and I did not. So I postponed plans to go out with friends and instead enjoyed two hours creating a black river with my mascara. Mom decided that this would be an opportune moment to explore the inner workings of her impressionable daughter and spent a long fifteen minutes questioning what had caused my reaction. My selfish pride made me to try to elude her questions, to escape the reality of my insecurity. But inevitably, I broke down and finally identified—only inwardly—that my life revolved around the fact that someone I dearly loved was the same person who caused me to think I had so little worth.

I once read a book that described all individuals as "peculiar treasures," unique gifts with particular abilities and talents who truly give of themselves. This inspired me, but when I was with Christine, I found my fear of inadequacy completely erased this mind-set. I had no talents; she had inherited them all. But there was always the fleeting thought that perhaps the world demanded something better, something superior, something that would require me to reach inside myself and pull out fiery passion.

This passion emerged a few years later, during my freshman year of high school. It first erupted during another significant conversation with my mother. It had been a particularly rough day followed by a particularly rough report card, and I didn't think that I could take it any longer, so I spilled it—I was sick of Christine. I was sick of being the last in line; I was sick of feeling like I couldn't do anything.

Mom, musing in a deep thoughtful manner that only mothers do, remembered: "You know, your sister feels the same way about you sometimes." Immediately, it seemed as though my anger discovered the loose brick in what previously was an endless wall, and I realized that my feelings were not only normal, but also shared by another.

Because of this simple statement, my angry heart initiated its healing, and I realized that I do have abilities. I do have talents, and I definitely do have something to give. Granted, there are days when Christine is prettier, smarter and more capable than I, but I have found them to be fewer and farther apart. Now, she is my partner, my friend and, most important, my big sister. I still have doubts and questions, but I think Shakespeare summed them up with one question: "Which can say more than this rich praise, that you alone are you?" ▣

Jerome

by Karly Ford

I sat hard on the plank of the porch step.
My mom sat a step above, her feet on my step
her legs, on each side of me, shone pale white against
  the yellow glow of the window and the night.

I wailed as she yanked through my hair with water
  and a short-toothed comb.

A bright pink bubble-gum ball had been syrupy sweet
until it managed to get lodged and matted in my curls.

My mom cried, too. She cried a lot since Jerome died.
None of us knew Jerome like she had,
  for nine months inside her.

Her fingers continued to pull the strands free,
  from scalp to tip, scalp to tip,
as if my bawling came from someone else.

Different Eyes

by Mary H. Wu

My best friend is Jennifer. Jennifer is all you could ask for in a friend. Not only is she funny, friendly, generous, sweet, lovable, sympathetic and talented, but she has a unique courage that no one can take from her.

Jennifer was born visually impaired. Usually the cornea covers the eye, allowing one to see clearly, but Jennifer's corneas are blurry and she can't see things well. To make matters worse, her hearing is not the best so she also needs hearing aids. But she doesn't let those things stop her from working hard and succeeding in life.

When Jennifer first went to school, she didn't realize that she had anything wrong with her eyes, but the other kids did and mocked her. They threw rocks and called her "Crooked Eyes." Kids are mean, plain and simple, and I feel sad that I wasn't around before second grade to defend her and yell back to leave her alone because my friend is so good. She didn't deserve abuse and torment. No one does.

I decided to help her now since I couldn't help her when she was little. I was placed in all her classes so I can be there to copy down all the notes from the blackboard since she can't see them. Her teachers enlarge her worksheets and tests. We do homework together and, while I zip through mine, I see her still working diligently on hers. And she pushes herself further. If it isn't neat enough, she writes the whole assignment over again. Sometimes, she types it. Other times she does projects weeks in advance and hands them in before anyone. Whenever she gets frustrated with the work, she never blames her sight. She doesn't say, "I hate God for doing this to me!" Instead, she says, "At least God gave me some sight, and that's all that matters."

Sometimes, when she isn't looking, I glance at Jennifer and wonder how she can manage to keep her head high when she hears everyone whisper excitedly about learning to drive. I wonder how she could not hate the people who once made fun of her. I wonder how she could not be angry at what she has. And, looking at her, struggling to understand and reading large-print papers and books, I sigh. She shouldn't have to struggle. She shouldn't have to keep her head high. She should be allowed to scream at the heavens for giving her this curse. But, she sees it not as a curse, but a blessing in disguise. She isn't angry at the world; she's happy with what she has.

Jennifer is my closest friend. I don't know what I'd do without her. I might help her academically, but she has helped me in so many ways. She's taught me that you don't have to have perfect vision to see what's going on. She views the world through her eyes, and it's clearer and more beautiful than anyone with 20/20 vision can see. Jennifer has taught me to laugh, to be carefree, to joke around, to take things as they come—and not to care what people think. She's taught me so much through how she sees the world.

Jennifer is not only my best friend, but she is a wonderful and talented human being. She is a strong individual who has faced the hurdles of life as they come. When she falls, she gets right up. When she hurts, she looks at what she *does* have. What she sees, we don't see. If we could see the world through Jennifer's eyes, we could see everything for what it really is, instead of what it appears to be. ▣

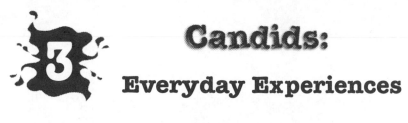

Candids:
Everyday Experiences

Photo by Alexa Schuler

Lonnie

by Gabrielle Rose Benadi

A light rain beats softly against my window. It's faint, like the long-lost conversations and memories that race through my head. Pushing back the bangs from my charcoal eyes, I stare into the glass reflection against night's black canvas. I glance around my bedroom, at my desk piled with schoolbooks, college applications, makeup, spare change and dusty frames with pictures of childhood playmates: my dog Sonny, my two younger sisters, my best friend Lonnie and me.

For a moment, I pause at a photo of Lonnie and me, our beaming smiles, her lanky arm draped around my neck. We looked like sisters with our waist-length chest-nut hair and matching green shirts. Most important, we looked happy. Judging from the photo, one could never guess that this friendship would ever die.

I have no explanation as to how I lost Lonnie or why best friendships end, although I can recognize the slow deterioration that takes place time and time again. There is a separation period when both people change their paths by meeting new people or staying home alone. Then they change their style of dress and borrow clothes from new friends. They use different expressions and their throats ring out a newly formed laughter.

Sitting next to Lonnie is uncomfortable, and standing behind her in line at the supermarket or guidance is not the same. Trivial comments that meant the world have reverted to the meaningless phrases they were meant to be. And little comments have grown into snide remarks as inside jokes are void of any giggles.

I could almost cry as I sit in the corner of my room wondering and searching for answers as to why. Was it something I did, or was it inevitable? Can we ever re-create the sturdy friendship we had or are we forever destined to be acquaintances with a friendship buried beneath memories? I feel a twinge of guilt for secretly being relieved of the heavy burden of Lonnie's extra, influential opinions and unwarranted advice I had to carry on my back.

Then my heart rolls into a tight little ball because I realize that Lonnie has no interest in the spider on my ceiling, the fight I just had with my parents or the smile *he* gave me Friday night at my new hangout where she has never been.

I question the perplexities of the situation as my low self-esteem kicks in, and I begin to wonder if maybe everything is fine and that I am imagining this or I am just under a lot of stress. Maybe she is under stress, too, or maybe her family is in the way, PSATs, SATs, junior ball, part-time jobs—all these minuscule wires that form a complex, barbed knot.

I decide to confront Lonnie and express my feelings. As fast as I pick up the phone, I hang it up because I don't have the faintest idea of what to say or how to start without sounding obnoxious, pathetic, possessive, mean, scared and hurt. What if she is unaware of the situation or decides to hang up? What if her egotistical boyfriend or her superficial friends are there? I decide to write a letter—it will give me the chance to state everything without being interrupted or nervous. Yet, there is the nagging fear that she might show it to someone or lose it, that maybe she'll laugh or be really hurt and cry, or she might twist the words like my knotted heart and once again obstruct our communication.

I play with my hair, twisting a curl around my finger and braiding the long piece in front like she did before her shiny hair was chopped. I remember holding her hand tight as her long tresses fell to the tiled floor of her mother's beauty salon. I smiled at her through soggy tissue, which filtered out the stench of permanent wave solution and told her I loved it even though I secretly hated it. Her fine hair had turned puffy like a large stick of cotton candy.

Abruptly, the shrill ringing of the phone, like distant laughter, awakens me from my daydream. I search for it now hiding beneath a rumpled red sweatshirt that I know she would never wear. Cautiously, I answer and am greeted by the singing voice of my *new* best friend. ▣

A Battle of Words

by Josh Stadtlander-Miller

The family is sitting down to eat, waiting for the meal to begin. Mom puts the food on the table and we all dig in. I am not very hungry, though I generally like my mother's cooking. I can feel the tension in the air; it is almost tangible. I dread these times that occur every two months during the school year. My report card is in, and so is my brother's. I am hoping that for once he will have good grades and my parents will be happy, but I can see the wrinkles in my mother's forehead. Her lips crack open, and she utters his name in the most menacing way possible.

"Do you have something to tell me about school?" she asks him. Sam responds by fidgeting and focusing on his food. She repeats the question.

"No, why?" Sam responds with anger and contempt.

Her eyes begin to redden as she asks me to pass the potatoes. I silently pretend to be more interested in eating than in what is going on around me. If I look interested, I know they will try to pull me into the conversation. I turn to see my cat, Pookie, look at me with huge, questioning eyes, meowing for me to pet her. I do, and she purrs.

I remember the food and begin to eat at the greatest

speed possible so I can leave and avoid the dreaded conversation. The food smells and tastes great. The chicken is moist with just the right amount of gravy, and the potatoes are steaming. I grab some salad and pour on my favorite Italian dressing. Then I hear Pookie jump down from the buffet table and meow. I give her a bit of chicken and return to my meal.

"Sam, if you don't pull your act together like your brother and start getting the grades I know you're capable of, I'm not going to let you have any privileges," Mom says as she gnaws on a bone.

I see my brother sinking lower into his chair cushion as he responds, "I am not my brother, and I did everything I was supposed to. I don't know why I didn't get better grades."

"We'll see if you did all that you were supposed to, because if you didn't, oh boy!" Mom is red in the face and looks like she's about to burst. I don't want to join in, but I feel like I have to or Mom will either kill Sam or explode. I know that once I utter any words, they will both try to use me as a defense in their argument.

Then Dad, who is also trying to avoid getting involved, interjects, "We know you're not Josh, and we don't expect you to be. We just expect you to try your best, and we can tell you have not been doing that." *Saved by Dad, thank goodness,* I think.

Mom says, "Your dad is right. You need to try as hard as you can."

"But I studied as much as possible. You can ask Josh; he saw me." At that, all eyes turn to me and I sink in my seat, trying to escape their gaze. I finish chewing and swallow hard. "Yeah, he was studying on, uh, Monday after school."

"How long was he studying?" Mom asks.

"How should I know?" I mumble.

"What did you say?"

"About thirty minutes, I think."

"Any other times?" my dad inquires.

"Not that I saw, but I don't exactly follow him around." I am very anxious saying this because I don't want to get him into any more trouble, but I realize I probably already have.

"On the weekend?"

"He was on the computer a long time." Oops, I shouldn't have said that. He is always playing, never working, on the computer.

"Ah ha! So you weren't studying, were you?"

"No, not then, but later," Sam looks at me with contempt, and I try to express my apologies by shrugging my shoulders.

"When later?"

"I don't remember."

Now that the conversation is not directed toward me, I can again fake interest in my food.

"Well, if you can't remember, then it must not have been very long."

"But I . . . ," he storms out of the room, tears in his eyes.

"Come back here!" I know that now my brother is in big trouble.

Dad angrily follows him, and my mom follows my dad, telling him to calm down. I take this opportunity to finish dinner and go downstairs to play my video game. I hear my brother crying, but I try to block it out. I am not able to listen to anyone in pain for long without intervening, so I go upstairs to defend his case, as usual. I know Sam is not physically harmed, but two-on-one, even in a battle of words, can be brutal, especially for a person who really has no case to defend. ▣

Photo by Amanda Jill Turkanis

Snow Angels

by Christine Susienka

The sting of the wind sharpens the rawness of my hands so that they become even more chafed and red. Tomato red. I pump them open and closed, trying to speed the circulation. My jeans are not waterproof, and the snow begins to seep through, numbing my legs. Splashes of sunlight stream into my eyes, but by pushing my cerulean-colored glasses back into place, I can see the shape of my best friend slide into focus. She leans over the top of the bleachers, snapping picture after picture of me as I slowly turn to ice while making angels in the snow. One look at her jawline, so set in concentration, and I burst out laughing.

"What?" she asks, the camera still clicking away as she leans farther over the rail. "Wait, don't answer; I want a picture of you laughing." I shake my head, amused by how ridiculous this whole scenario is and wondering how I ever ended up in it. Then I realize that I wouldn't trade this moment for anything.

"That *should* be enough," Sarah-Neel calls down to me. "Now get up slowly so that I can shoot the whole process." I do, being careful not to ruin any of the shapes I've created. She is moving down the bleachers, taking a few at a time and playing with the camera.

"Now, let's look. I must've taken, like, eighty." I meet her at the bottom, brushing the snow off my clothes as she pushes a series of buttons, then pushes them again. She raises her eyes to meet mine. "Where are they?" she asks.

"What do you mean, 'Where are they?' I'm freezing, soaked through, and probably going to catch pneumonia, and you didn't even take the pictures?" I exclaim with enough sarcasm that she knows my anger's not genuine.

She reaches into her pocket and pulls out her pair of green gloves. "I'm sorry. Would you like a glove?" she asks, sliding one onto her own small hand and offering me the other.

"Yes," I laugh, snatching it and immediately feeling the reassuring tingling running through my fingers. I don't have frostbite—not yet anyway.

"Oh wait, here they are! But there are only six," she cries out, a slight look of triumph on her face.

"I thought you said you took eighty!" I exclaim.

"I did. I pushed the button at least that many times!"

"What happened?"

"I don't know. Here, look." She hands me the digital camera and I use the viewer to see myself sprawled in the snow.

"Hey, these aren't too bad," I am pleased to discover, "except, yuck, get rid of this one." I try to delete the image, but she wrestles the camera from me.

"I like it," she presumptuously declares.

"Just like that one I've got of you . . . that Adam would love to see."

Her face drains of color as she shakes her head. "You wouldn't dare."

I say nothing, but my raised eyebrows and plotting smile speak for me. She promptly deletes the picture that I do not like.

"What time is it?" I ask.

"About quarter to four. We've still got time before your mom gets here. Let's go warm up. I'm cold."

"You're cold? You're not even the one who's been lying in the snow," I comment.

"I was perfecting my photography skills. It's very strenuous."

I push her playfully and she falls into a snowbank; her wild vermilion hair is in stark contrast to the whiteness. She doesn't stay there long before jumping to her feet and sending a snowball flying in my direction. I duck and laugh, making some comment about her bad aim to which she responds by shoving me into the snow. I clamber to my feet and brush clumps of snow from my hair. "Is that really the best you can do?" I taunt, challenging her, and within minutes we're both on the ground again, laughing and looking at the sky. It's one of those ethereal skies rich in shades of blue and bands of sunlight that stream through the clouds in just the right way so that you know it couldn't come from anywhere but heaven.

We sit there for a few moments, but then continue down the path and hurriedly step into her house, shaking off the snow. Neither of us thought to wear boots, so our socks and feet are quite wet, our toes numb and shriveled, but we don't care. Trudging into the kitchen, we immediately start making massive cups of hot chocolate with every flavoring we can find. Peppermint. Almond. Vanilla. Raspberry. Then we climb the stairs to her room and plop ourselves on the bed, mugs in hand. The steam drifts in fragrant wisps and we inhale the scent, not speaking.

I look around me. White paper lanterns in a scattering of shapes hang from the ceiling. A Picasso graces one wall, photographs another. A few of them are of me. I remember when they were taken—the party last summer, the dance, the beach. I smile as I remember. Interesting knickknacks are everywhere. It is a comfortable room, one that makes you feel at home. If there is such a thing as being entirely comfortable with yourself, then Sarah-Neel is it.

I study her features as she gazes out the window. The set jawline. The dazed look of someone lost in thought. Then I study her clothes. They barely match, they're wrinkled, and they're three sizes too big, and yet somehow they work. They make her look like, well, her. Something shakes her from her daze, and she jerks her head up sharply, sending me a quick smile.

"You know, you're the only one I can do this with. Just sit here, do nothing, and be completely happy without worrying whether you're happy doing the same thing." I glance at her and don't say anything, merely absorbing what she has said. She's the only one I can talk to about anything, come up with crazy things to do, or make angels in the snow with.

"What would we do without each other?" she asks finally, with complete sincerity.

"We'd be lost," I respond, only half-joking. ◙

Thanks, but No Thanks

by Nicole K. Press

Thanksgiving

The holiday of thanks
  But why, tell me,
    Is there no holiday,
    No day declared,
    No day solely for the purpose
Of thanks,
But no thanks?

Of thanks for not helping me
  When I needed you most.
Thanks so much for not backing me up
  When you knew I was right.
  Thanks for keeping secrets
  Thanks for pretending
  For betraying,
  Lying,
  For being you,

And not who I thought you were.
Perhaps the third Wednesday in November
  Should be a day of truth
Then you would know
  What you truly have
  To be thankful for.

What's Important

by Jason Friedman

he guy on TV took a monster kick square on the chin. His head jerked back, blood spilling out of his mouth all over the stark white mat, and he fell with a solid thud. My dad and I cringed. "Ouch," I said.

The guy sitting next to Van Damme turned to him and said, "That's why they call it bloodsport, man."

I groaned, disgusted. My dad twisted his face into a gruesome expression of mock agony, which he held momentarily before we both burst out in laughter. I hit him full force in the face with a couch pillow. "Ow!" he said, laughing. "What was that for?"

"Hey," I retorted, "that's why they call it bloodsport."

Watching bad movies with Dad is always great, because we have the same sense of humor, so we think the same things are funny. It seems as though we're always laughing.

My parents are very good about avoiding conflicts, mostly because they remember what it was like to be seventeen. Sometimes. They rarely lecture me on family values or tell me "this is right" or force me to do anything, really. They recognize what's going to get me ticked and usually find a good way to navigate a touchy issue. Usually.

Even if they don't lecture, they can impart their values clearly enough in our everyday conversations. Most of what they tell me I can figure out on my own, but I've found one pervading idea in everything they do or say: family. Being with family is what's important to them, and therefore to me. That's why we have big Thanksgiving dinners and Passover seders with the whole family every year. That's why my parents were so upset when my aunt and uncle and cousins moved to California, because they thought they were running out on the family. That's why we try to take at least one family vacation every year. Because you only have so much time with your family, and, as I grow, clearly my time is starting to run out.

Which isn't to say that my parents don't have values, or that they don't lay them on me. Actually, they're quite good at it.

"You know what we need?" I asked.

We were sitting downstairs—my mom, my dad and I. My sister was upstairs studying for a midterm. Studying is important.

We usually eat dinner together but tonight Mom had a class, and with midterms, everyone is basically eating on individual schedules, so we called in for pizza. Good pizza is important. Now, after dinner, Mom and Dad were eating leftover Chinese food, and I was drinking orange juice. Eating dinner together is important, but studying and Mom's classes are important, too.

"You know what we need?" I repeated.

"His face looks great. Doesn't it look great?" Mom asked my dad, referring to my ongoing battle with acne in which I am gaining an upper hand. Acne is important. They remind me every day.

"It really does. You having sex with Amanda or something?" Amanda is my girlfriend. Girlfriends are important. Dad told me that. Many times.

Shock spread quickly across Mom's face. "What?! You better not be having sex with Amanda. You're both jailbait." No premarital sex. VERY important.

"I better stop then. You know what we need?" Finally I had their attention. "Shot glasses."

My dad laughed.

"Yeah. Shot glasses. I want to do juice shots."

"Okay," Mom said. "I'll find a shot glass for you." Orange juice. Important.

Van Damme wins another match of the *kumite,* and the movie yields in favor of a commercial. I hit Dad with another pillow. Chaos ensues.

After two minutes of a wrestling brawl, we slump on the couch, shaking with laughter, trying to catch our breath.

"Do you have a meet on Sunday?" he asks me.

"I don't know. Probably not." He makes a face. "Sorry. Why?"

"Mom wants me to go to the museum on Sunday," he says, frowning. Museums. Definitely not important.

I'm going to college next year, so there probably won't be too many more couch-pillow fights or talks about orange-juice shots and sex with sixteen-year-old girls. *I'll miss them,* I think. That's family. Important. Yeah, I'll miss it. But that's life. That's why they call it bloodsport. ▣

Leaving the Club

Fiction by Holly M. Kuczynski

In the club, there is no ebony darkness or crystalline illumination, just a tangled silvery atmosphere, matted flat and pressed against cool, strange-smelling air. I can barely make out the neon sign above the bar; it radiates electric yellow as it flickers behind a dense veil of fumes spewing from the dry-ice machines packed tightly in the corners. Black leather-clad dancers stomp and parade aggressively on the foggy dance floor. The ice fumes curl and ripple beneath their feet like ivory clouds torn apart by a storm.

"Why do people keep writing this awful, depressing music? It's terrible." Jed is beside me, musing agitatedly about the heavy, blasting music. "If they hate their lives so much, why don't they quit and do the economy some good?" he drones, but I don't pay attention. There is too much glitter pulsating before my eyes.

Kelli is leaning against Jed. She has green-apple hair, midback length and shimmery, like the concoction sloshing in the fluted glass resting on her bare knee. She has long, tigerlike nails painted a trashy yellow that don't coordinate well with her muddy green halter top. She smokes pretty, violet-colored cigarettes that reek of a tasteless dime-store quality and believes that they somehow give her strength. I disagree and, so, often tell her.

The Goth set leaves the floor. Mysterious, vampirelike beings slink toward the bar, drawn by the aura of that erratic yellow neon whose sparks are lost within the residue of dozens of cheap cigarettes.

In the sea of smoke, punks are slamming around. The muted din of bodies colliding echoes over the hyperactive screams and rants of a band I've never heard of. I watch the pit of bodies and all I see are arms and legs, flailing and distorted, that don't seem to belong to anyone in particular. They remind me of motorized mannequins, the ones with no eyes but staticky red curls. I murmur these thoughts to Iris, who is sitting beside me on the worn velvet couch.

Iris does not seem to be paying attention, so I stop. She has not been the same since she stopped eating, since she decided to unlatch the box deep inside her mind and release the voices that she says whisper beautiful, sophisticated things. They are malicious things that penetrate and dissolve even the most persevering common sense.

Sometimes when I look at her I want to cry, because she is not immortal like she thinks she is. She says that someday she will be as light as an angel—weightless enough to fly. She will be flesh molded onto bone with nothing in between. I imagine that there must be bruising, purplish veins tangled around the crumbling ivory pillars that make up her very being. I can almost see all of this beneath her pale skin.

I unravel her. Pulling back every translucent layer, I watch as that sophisticated facade shrivels up beyond the point of revival. And I know that even though she speaks of the future when she says she will be beautiful, today weighs heavily on her bony shoulders. Her home life is so dismal it chases her out to places like this and other places I prefer not to think about.

I wonder how she can carry it all when she's so empty inside. That is what I think, that she is hollowed out and emotionless. Iris has grown dark to the point where no light can touch her. She is choosing to give up on everything that used to mean so much to her.

Iris whispers about losing all hope in her future because she is afraid of destiny. I fear my destiny, too, sometimes. Other times, I wish I could peer into the future, if only for a second. But I am afraid of what I would be. I am afraid I would turn out like Iris's mother, bound in a loveless marriage with self-destructive habits that cause her to leak more of her soul than her thin flesh can hold. I am afraid of Iris becoming like her. But I cannot say this. There is no way to tell your friend that you think her mother is trash.

The strobe lights are flashing. I feel hypnotized and nauseated. Iris is still whispering tumultuous words that carve indentations into my mind. I want to close my mind, but I cannot, because I feel that I am in the middle of some nightmare where it is not easy to stop thinking. And so many thoughts rush at me at once. I realize I am trapped inside a box, one that holds death and desire so well blended that neither is distinguishable to the naked eye.

I need to leave. I stand, closing my eyes suddenly and trying not to be sick over everything that is going on around me. I need to run away to some place meant for people like me, a place full of people who are not afraid of the dark, but sometimes need light. I wish Iris could come with me, and we could just hang out all day and talk about boys and dreams and the animal shapes that clouds create.

Jed and Kelli are lounging all over each other. They are snickering and sipping some dark liqueur that reminds me of the thickest, smoothest black satin, the kind you can imagine would stain your fingertips if you touched it. They have long since given up on school and real friends, on trust and emotions. I think there are times when everyone wishes to be a hero, and this is my time. I take Iris by her wrist, which feels like a cold metal pole. I drag her out of the room and pull her down the long hallway to the exit, rushing and trying not to trip over the hem of my black skirt.

We emerge from the underground darkness, and tendrils of white smoke curl out. Iris hasn't asked what we are doing or where we are going, but I tell her I am going to take her somewhere better, a place without pretended ugliness, plastic people and broken dreams. I want to make her well again. I want to feed her life, the kind drenched with hope and raw emotion that can fill you up completely, but still make you yearn for more. I wonder what she is thinking, but I do not ask. She is staring up at the dark night sky. There are tiny diamonds glued to the dark ribbon of shimmering silk wrapped around a crescent moon. I wonder where the other part of the moon is. I hope that I always think like this. I want to think clearly and smoothly, like liquid diamonds coating my eyes.

I will dream tonight. I will dream about Iris and the club. I will not be able to help the demons that invade my dreams, but I will not run away from them either. And I hope that Iris will do the same. 回

Art by Merideth Finn

Crazy Love

by Jessica L. Bethoney

A grapefruit, I decided. She's shaped like a grapefruit with a witch's snowy hair. Her painted nails drummed on the violet tablecloth, and her gaudy bracelets clanged together. Her bony fingers clutched the cross dangling from her neck. Aunt Carol turned her crinkled face toward her four children. Mary was gorgeous in her wedding dress. Chris danced gaily with his newest girlfriend. For the moment he was sober and able to mask his gambling addiction. Marie danced with her new boyfriend and their baby, her alcoholic ex-husband now in her past. Dave, the schizophrenic, sat motionless in his chair. Her fifth child, Joe, had been killed in a motorcycle accident at nineteen, but his picture was the religious brooch pinned to Aunt Carol's blouse.

Suddenly, Aunt Carol tuned into the conversation behind her. "Braces are expensive, but Michael will need them," my mother complained to Aunt Dee.

"God knows you don't need braces, Michael," Aunt Carol cried out. Dad and Michael, my younger brother, exchanged glances, their bemused smiles saying what was on my mind. "Yeah, all you hafta do is twist your tooth a little bit every night, and it'll straighten out! Who needs braces?" she shrieked with a mad laugh, stuffing a handful of nuts into her painted mouth. A few nuts fell onto her dress, which she violently brushed away with a napkin. "Damn nuts," she muttered.

Michael mused aloud, clearly confused, "Yeah, but then my tooth would fall out!"

"No! If you do it right, it will work!" Aunt Carol confidently replied. Disgusted, my cousin Debbie flung down her napkin and walked away with a snort. My fingers wound around the table like vines, slowly turning my knuckles pale, and my knees began to shake. Everyone at the table laughed apprehensively. Aunt Dee quickly changed the subject.

"So, um, where did you purchase Mary's dress, Carol? It's lovely! I was helping Kathleen shop for a wedding dress the other day, and we found an exquisite one at a flea market, but we didn't buy it. I've been regretting it all week."

"Oh, no, don't be sorry. That dress was probably cursed. You never want to buy used wedding dresses; they carry evil spirits," Aunt Carol ended with her insane laugh. Fidgeting, I excused myself and walked to the bathroom on unsteady legs.

How odd she is, I thought to myself. *Such a strange woman, and yet a survivor.* I pictured Aunt Carol as a child. Abandoned by her alcoholic parents, she dutifully took responsibility for her siblings while hiding in a school. Later, she was bounced between foster homes. After marrying, she moved to the Cape with her five children and husband to open a souvenir shop, only to go bankrupt. Her abuse of alcohol, the death of her son, her entire past . . . too much of a burden for one woman to endure . . . even with the solace of the church.

I remembered horrible tales I had heard about Aunt Carol from family members. "She used to come to gatherings so drunk she was blind." "She's a crazed lunatic." "She used to tell Darrell if he'd just concentrate, the voices would go away. What he needed was professional help."

Then, memories of my childhood visits at her house drifted back. The moment I entered her kitchen I would be enveloped in a hug, and she would cackle. She'd hand me an immense plate piled high with my favorite Lebanese foods, although the meat would sometimes be raw. "You don't need to cook it. It's top-quality beef, so it won't harm you," she'd state firmly. As I left, she'd proclaim, "God bless you," her sole expression of love. It seemed to give her support during the rough times to think God would someday bless her.

Gaining my composure, I walked back to where goodbyes were being exchanged. "Congratulations! We'll see you soon, Aunt Carol," I called.

"God bless you, sweetheart. Give me a kiss. I'll see you soon."

"See ya, Aunt Carol." I spun around and headed toward the exit. My lips curled in a rueful smile, and I peered over my shoulder at her. She was shoving the leftover dessert nuts into her pockets. As she turned around to wave, her pockets sagged, and nuts spewed onto the floor.

"Crazy, but I love her," I decided, shaking my head as I stepped into the car. "Crazy love." ▣

Ohio

by Amber Bard

going on vacation—
drive might take a while
so i pack up my expensive cds
my expensive cd player
pack up my expensive clothes

getting there, driven forever
sanity fleeing more after each city
but we're going around to some different towns now
ones i've never seen
maybe the boredom will pass
the scenery is so different here:
buildings half torn apart
looking like something in an ad on tv
for some war-torn country
far, far away from my flag-hoisting country

kids as young as ten
skating through cracked sidewalks
on old, worn-out boards
old punk band stickers scraped and faded to an outline
some have cigarettes stuck behind their ears
most are mistaking them for pacifiers

i think, those should be suckers—
those should be cherry suckers

we stop at a red light
(damn light, my mother says)
looking out of an open window
i wave at a man smoking in his car on the street
(don't wave at strangers, my dad snaps irritably—
especially from this neighborhood)
this man has lauryn hill turned up
even louder than my screeching noise
i wonder, is it the differing cultures?
or just two different tastes?
i wave again, trying to look sweet
he turns to me with a sad look on his face
and swivels around angrily
without waving back—
did this town make him so harsh?

i race by buildings with holes in roofs
in my mother's white grand am
an ancient man is riding past us
on his rickety bicycle
and i wish he had a white car too

small children with dirty faces
they crawl all over their tired mother
i wouldn't mind watching her children for a while
so she might soak her feet and paint her nails
like my mom does
maybe she could even learn to rest a while

none of this is noticed by my parents
who sit in the front, arguing once again
about the fastest way to our destination
i don't think they want to stay in this place for long
i think they want to speed by it, forgetting it
safe from America in the sanctuary of leather seats
and metal walls covered in attractive retouchable white
   paint

my attention diverted from the trivial happenings
   of the front seat,
i glance to my right
a young man is scurrying out of a homemade shelter
plastic and cardboard and crates
his shirt bears the same name as the cd in my
   expensive player:
Dead Kennedys.
the singer screams with agony about cambodia
and reagan while i shakily realize
that could be me
me

but not quite
not for real
i would have my parents
my parents' visa, my parents' concern.
and this boy has nothing but cardboard.
where am i.
this can't be america.
this cannot be the land of opportunity,
   land of low unemployment,

land of magic.
this little town in ohio impacts me more
than any adopt-this-skinny-child-from-biafra
*   magazine ad.*

cardboard, cigarettes, cynicism:
proud to be an american.

Photo by Schuyler Coppedge

Trip Down Pacific Highway

by Jennifer Maberry

The sun came streaming in the open top of the convertible that Saturday. The wind swept through my hair, whipping the loose pieces against my cheeks. My dad looked suave behind the wheel, in a baseball cap and a pair of Foster Grants, not the fatherly attire I was accustomed to. The Pacific Ocean chased us on the right, and the rocky cliffs of Malibu separated us from the rest of the world. We sat there in silence, soaking in the salty aroma wafting from the ocean, thinking.

"Beautiful day, isn't it?" he asked pensively. I nodded. He reached over and turned on the radio. "You know," he shouted, trying to compete with the suddenly intrusive music. "When I was a kid," I rolled my eyes in anticipation, "we never went on any vacations, especially not to California."

"And you walked five miles to school, uphill, both ways," I added. He smiled. I turned and gazed at the jagged cliff side, remembering when I was five years old and asked him to marry me. He explained that he was already married to Mommy, but I was still his best girl. Those were the times I thought my dad was the handsomest man in the world.

Then, I became a teenager, and suddenly Daddy wasn't the most important or best-looking man in my life. Brad Pitt, who still makes my top five, bumped Dad off the list. At my thirteenth birthday party, he attempted the Macarena in front of my friends. I was so embarrassed I wanted to crawl under a rock and die.

With my sixteenth birthday came the privilege that kids wait for their entire lives—driving. Our white car could be seen every Sunday afternoon, driving in large, shaky circles around the school parking lot.

"Remember," he would say, grasping the seat with white knuckles, "this is not a race. Take your time and don't hesitate to use the brake; that's what it's there for." This ritual went on for some time until I got good enough to go out on the road. I have never seen him look so terrified, except when we came home from summer vacation and our grass was brown and missing in spots.

Now that I'm almost an adult, I guess Dad plays a new role in my life. Although I am not the chubby little redhead who couldn't go to sleep until her daddy came to kiss her good night, I will always be his "Jennifer, Jennifer baby mennifer," a term of endearment whose origin or meaning neither of us remembers.

I felt the smooth motion of the road under the car jump as it slowed to a stop. He was staring intently at the road, his eyes focused on the car in front of us. I looked up at the sky and felt the warm rays of the sun beat down upon us.

"It is a beautiful day, isn't it?" I said. He smiled and nodded. ▣

West Meets East

by Janine B. Lee

My mom stood in the living room cleaning our white porcelain Buddha. Like some dust-busting Xena, she shot a spritz of Fantastik onto its bald head and wiped it vigorously with an old T-shirt. Then she focused her cleaning talent on the dusty terra-cotta robes of Jesus, moved onto Mary's blue veil and then decided Buddha's head wasn't shiny enough after all.

Wow, I thought. *I guess we lost more money in the stock market than I realized.* As I walked through my house, I began to assess our family's financial status by applying a theory I had developed long ago—the cleaner the house during the off-holiday season, the more debts we owe. I carefully opened our fridge, prepared to catch any pig intestines, fish heads or soy sauce packets ready to fall from an overstuffed, Chinese refrigerator. But I didn't have to catch anything between my knees. All I had to do was blink into the light of the fridge (which I hadn't seen for over two years) and wonder that I could actually see space between the milk and the economy-sized tub of margarine. Yep, it was time to start deep-frying onion rings at that fast-food spot again.

But if a clean refrigerator was the worst of it, at least it would hardly be unusual (to normal families, that is). In the middle of my dining table, I saw a bright orange porcelain fish leaping into the air. On the walls, I saw gold and red signs of the Chinese character xi hung upside down. And the mirrors were covered with white sheets. Had Amy Tan decided to come over and redecorate my house? Then my gaze fell upon the culprit innocently lying on the couch—a book titled *The Art of Feng Shui*. I doubled over with laughter. *She'll come to her senses soon,* I thought.

I thought wrong. The following week, my mom decided at 1:00 A.M. that my bed was placed in a bad Feng Shui position.

"Nin, wake up," my mother whispered fiercely in Chinese. "Your bed is not supposed to face the door."

"What do you want me to do? Move it now?" I replied groggily.

"Just turn your body around for now so your feet face the door and not your head," she said, slapping my leg to make me obey.

"Ow, ow, all right, all right," I groaned. I turned my body around and fell back onto the bed, pulling the covers back over me.

But my mom still didn't leave me alone. "Nin! One more thing!" I heard her say.

"What now?" came my muffled voice.

"Tomorrow I want you to clean the fish tank downstairs and get rid of those black angel fish. They're no good. Go buy some big, fat goldfish."

At that point, I really thought I was dreaming. "What? I just can't flush those fish down the toilet!" I yelled.

"Just return them," she said calmly.

"I bought those fish two years ago!"

"Then give them to someone," she replied matter-of-factly. Alright, that was it. It was time to confront her about these absurdities. I jumped out of bed, flicked on the light and squinted at her.

"Mom, don't you think this is getting stupid? You're a woman with a graduate degree and a career, not some mother from *The Joy Luck Club*," I said, trying to reason with her.

She didn't say anything.

I switched gears and hit her where I knew it would hurt. "And aren't you a Christian? I thought you were supposed to place your faith in God, not these dumb superstitions." She looked a little sheepish.

"And do you really think this is going to help us get our money back or pay my way through college?"

Then she just looked sad and her eyes became bleak. I had more to say, but I couldn't go on when I saw her expression. She seemed so hopeless. She got up quietly and left.

I turned the light off and wondered, *What had that accomplished? I just got my mom really depressed. But at least she's not living in la la land. She's got to face reality,* I argued with myself.

Then I had an epiphany of sorts, but in the form of that MasterCard commercial. Goldfish: $2.00. Chinese signs: $1.50. Housecleaning: $0. Peace of mind: priceless. Reason is cold comfort. Besides, the world doesn't make much sense. I decided to buy some goldfish. ▣

Breaking Tradition

by Stacey Zabusky

"tacey, will you be home for dinner tonight?" my mother shouts from downstairs.

"Um, I'll let you know," I shout from my room. Even though I can't see her, I know she is frustrated. I can't understand why; you would think that after four years of having this conversation every Friday she would be used to my noncommittal response.

My family has always eaten Friday night dinner together for the start of the Jewish Sabbath. When I was younger, I looked forward to the special meal Mom spent all afternoon cooking. The smell of chicken soup would fill the house with such a delicious aroma that my stomach would grumble as soon as I stepped in the house. I would wait all week to see what interesting way my mom would cook the traditional chicken or what variation of potatoes (my dad's favorite) she would serve. If I was lucky, she would ask my opinion on the meal, so I was sure to get what I wanted.

Each week I would lift the tall, silver candlesticks out of the glass breakfront and place them on the table, then wait anxiously until I heard my father arrive home. Then I would race to the small drawer where he kept his yarmulkes and carefully choose one for him to wear.

There was the worn brown velvet one from his wedding and the blue one with white polka dots I had made, but my favorite was black velvet with rainbow swirls. After shoving the rest back into the drawer, I would race down and proudly hand it to him.

Next came the blessing over the wine, which my father chanted in a loud, clear voice. We would join in when he reached a certain point. My youngest sister would say the blessing over the challah bread, and I would get to cut it and hand it out.

Then came the delicious meal I had waited for all week. As soon as we finished, my sisters and I would race to turn on the TV. Somehow my sister would manage to drag my father into the room, too, and we would have an evening of family bonding . . . until recently.

At seventeen, the last thing I want to do on a Friday night is have family dinners and bonding time. I'd rather go out for pizza than eat chicken; I'd rather see a movie than watch TV; I'd rather choose an outfit for myself than a yarmulke for my father.

Each week I am torn between my family duties and my desire to go out and have fun. I know how happy it makes my parents if I eat dinner with them, but I love to go out! Sometimes I do both, and sometimes I go out and skip dinner. But I know these traditions will always be with me, and one day I will probably have the same conflict with my own children. ▣

Leaning on Each Other

by Rebecca Rae Bodfish

he breeze gently stirred the white curtains, filling my nose with the pungent aroma of a late summer afternoon.

Kate and I sat side-by-side leaning against my parents' bed, watching TV and occasionally talking. The pauses in our chatter were not filled with tension but rather a comfortable silence that happens between good friends.

A commercial that we both hated came on, so the silence was broken by our jokes and groans as we proceeded to make fun of the cartoon dancing across the screen. As the advertisement ended, the shrill ring of the telephone quieted us momentarily. I lunged for it.

Kate turned her attention back to the television, but soon focused on me as my voice became less audible and my shoulders slumped forward.

I gripped the phone tightly, as if it were the one thing that would keep me from breaking down. My knuckles turned white. My breathing was shallow and came in little gasps as I tried desperately to consume the oxygen I had lost from holding my breath.

"Me, too," I murmured one last time before placing the phone in its cradle.

I felt Kate's arm tentatively touch my shoulder. I

squeezed my eyes tight, trying to get control and not let the tears that were so close to the surface overtake me.

Kate moved so we were face-to-face and embraced me. I clung to her for support as the tears were unleashed. We stood that way for five minutes before she gently stepped back to look at me.

"What happened?" Although her voice was soft, it boomed in the silence.

"My dad was admitted to the hospital. They don't know what's wrong, but it has to do with his heart." My voice was shaking, but I made no effort to steady it.

By some unspoken understanding, we sat back down to watch TV, leaning against each other for support instead of the bed. The shadows of the evening no longer seemed refreshing; they spoke of dark things hiding and waiting to be revealed.

I moved closer to Kate, grateful for her presence on such a cold summer's night. ▣

Photo by Kellie Smith

Portraits:
Of Moms and Dads

Photo by Susan E. Ogar

My Mother's Hands

by Dan Feng Mei

Many things touch the heart—a snowflake in a storm, a leaf falling in autumn. My mother has touched my heart. In her eyes, I see her undying desire to learn and in her hands, her struggle to raise her family. I admire her spirit and the power of her hands.

I can imagine her as a little girl with long black hair in a ponytail, walking to school along the grassy sidewalks of China. She carries a school bag her grandmother sewed for her, and her shoes have a brown stain that sets her apart from her classmates. She drags her feet through the muddy streets, occasionally looking up at the sun for comfort; she has not had breakfast. I hear coins jingling in her coat pocket; she's finally saved a month's worth of lunch money for school tuition. Today, she will have to start saving again for next semester.

Sometimes I wake up in the middle of the night and see light coming from the bathroom. My mother struggles to read the two-week-old newspaper, eyelids drooping and hands relaxing. But somehow she manages to keep reading, absorbing knowledge.

I can feel the contour of my mother's fingers when I think of her. The tips are cracked from constantly washing white rice and green vegetables. Scrubbing clothes has added years of texture. Her job as a seam-stress has made her fingers stiff, yet she goes to the fac-tory, day after day, and sews. On rainy days, she asks me to wash the rice for her, saying she has to do something else. But I know better—her hands ache on rainy days.

I look at my mother and see her white hair and the eyes that looked to the sun for relief from hunger. The worn-out hands continue to scrub and wash; her fine skin is aging rapidly. Although some see my mother as a woman with bad eyesight, rough, man-like hands and little education, I see her as an exceptional person with qualities I hope to have one day. ▣

Tell Me a Story

by Justine M. Forrest

My father and I are driving down a road where the trees filter the sun from my view. We are silent. I glance quickly at him. One of his tan hands rests on the steering wheel; the other is on his chin. He must be thinking. I turn my gaze out the window. My older sister sits motionless in the back. We have made this trip more than a thousand times, yet today is different. I just asked my dad to tell us what he was like when he was young. He has shared a couple of stories, some I'd heard a million times, and others are new.

"Hey, Dad," I look at him. This is one of the first times I realize he's getting old. We just celebrated his fortieth birthday and his black curly hair seems to have grayed overnight. His expressions are just like they were when I was little, only right now, his face is blank. Something is making a noise. I shake off my daydream; it's my Dad.

"J, are you okay?"

"Of course, Dad. Was I saying something?" I reply, searching to figure out what I was trying to say. Then I remember, "Will you tell me the story about you and the snowballs?"

My dad knew which story I meant since I have asked

to hear it so many times. "All right, let me see. From the beginning?" my dad asks.

I nod in approval.

"Well, I was with a few of my friends, Billie, John and Frank. We played football and baseball together, so we prided ourselves on our amazing aim. Although, you must remember that this is an eight-year-old's amazing aim, so it may not have been that good. But still, I practiced all the time. Anyway, we loved wintertime, especially the snow. We had snowball wars all the time. Sometimes we threw snowballs at passing cars. This was not very smart, and I do not recommend it because it's very unsafe." He always added some lesson.

"We're lucky we didn't cause an accident. The snowballs were meant to hit the front windshields; whether they did or not is another story. Usually, the people in the car didn't get out; they were just annoyed. But if they ever did, each of us had an escape route.

"One time this red Camaro sped by. I picked up my ammunition and released it at precisely the right time. The snowball landed exactly on the driver's side of the window. Direct hit! Perfect. The next thing I knew, the sporty car screeched to a halt. The angry driver threw open his car door and ran toward me. My friends and I dropped our white bombs and started for our escape routes. Clearly, the man was after me. I started sprinting to the fence, jumped over it, under the tree, over another fence, through a backyard. All the while, I could hear his footsteps gaining. I kept running as fast as I could. Then I heard a choking sound and the footsteps stopped. The clothes wire that I ducked under stopped the man. He must have run into it. I heard the man get up slowly and go back. That incident curtailed my snowball throwing."

My sister and I chuckle as we picture our dad being chased by a madman. I decide to find out more. "What was your life like growing up?" My dad always says my life is too fast, but I don't agree. It was ironic when next he said that very thing.

"Slower than yours by a mile. I think that I spent almost every hour of daylight outside playing games. We had a street full of kids, and we played all the time. The TV had only three channels: 2, 4, and 7. There were no malls. Depending on the season, I would play basketball behind my house, football down the street, baseball at school. I started caddying golf when I was ten years old and made ten dollars a day for carrying a bag eighteen holes twice. I loved that. Most summers I would leave the house in the morning and not return until well after dark." He stopped a moment, remembering something.

"I can remember taking showers at night to wash off a day's grime, and having my calf muscles ache because I walked around the golf course so many times or played so many games. I did not have many responsibilities, except maybe taking out the trash Monday nights. Of course, I objected often and loudly, but I did it. I did not sit still much."

Again, I tried to picture my dad's life. It must have been so much fun—being outside and basically carefree. I wonder if that's when his love of golf began. His dedication has propelled him to win many tournaments.

Out my window, I see a family walking, which makes me think of some of my most favorite memories with my dad. I wonder if his are the same. "Dad, what was the best time in your life?" I wait for his response.

He must really be thinking because he doesn't answer for a while.

Then he replies, "I do not look at my life in terms of best times and worst times. Instead, I think that I am on a journey, an evolution of my soul. I need the good things and the bad things to help define my path.

"I can tell you the times when I feel most fulfilled. Spending time with my children is by far the best for me. It is one of a very few occasions when I am calm and living in the moment. Just being in the car with you guys. I think our purpose in life is to love and to give of ourselves. It is in the giving that we realize the most joy. In a sense, it is in the giving that we become immortal. Think about all of our stories, about Browney and Whitey."

My dad used to make up stories about how my sister's and my stuffed animals would come alive and save the day. "And reading Nancy Drew, think about how much time we spent. I bet you never went to sleep in less than thirty minutes each night. Those times together are ones I can instantly relive. They will stay with me until I die, and I believe they will stay with you."

Tears form in my eyes. I turn my gaze back out the window as we pull into my mom's driveway; the hour and a half with Dad is over. I'm home now. ▣

Eight Minutes
by Christine Loftus

I bought an ugly, cheap, worthless watch with a fake
name brand from an ugly, cheap, worthless vendor
on a filthy New York City street.
I knew immediately it had some inexplicable authority
over me.
And it took advantage.
It tortured me,
With every metal device of which it was formed,
Every link and hook and both hands turning.
It gave me eight minutes to practice as I waited
for your arrival.
Words were clear and perfect in my mind,
A speech prepared, with the most perfect words.
As the second hand returned to its starting point
after eight laps around, you appeared.
And as I lifted my jeweled wrist to touch you,
my words slithered away.
I lost the conflict, the will to speak.
And I'll never escape the fear of that second hand,
Or the effortless way you prevented my words.
My little clock still regrets, still remembers how long
I waited to tell you
How Mom felt when you tempted her.

With a vision of color and brilliance
A vision of white, like a wedding dress,
And when you prevented something you saw
  so beautifully,
She was swallowed by black and digested.
And she hasn't recovered yet.
But you'll never know this.
Or that I can never, ever give my hand to someone
  to hold for fear they will
Prevent my vision or tempt me with something greater
  than I can expect,
But I trust myself. So I am selfish, I suppose.
And you were late.
And I never told you.
This slinky circle of cold steel froze my words.
But the most valuable possession I ever owned was
  that time,
A solid eight minutes of power and purpose and pride.

Photo by Kelly Gibson

So Much Alike

by Danielle Marie Bourassa

 *'est qui lui? Et puis elle c'est qui?"* My mother asked about my teachers as we walked by the classrooms.

"Mon professeur d'algebre de l'année passée, et elle, elle était mon prof de biologie," I answered. Some friends came up to say hello, and my mother quickly switched to English, though with a thick accent. I watched her closely. Her blonde and gray hair was messily pulled into a bun, as was mine. Her eyes smiled, lighting up her face and accenting the familiar wrinkles that pleated as she laughed. We moved to the next room of the open house to hear the update from teachers who were routine to me, but so novel to her.

I looked at her as Mr. Frank talked. We sat the same way, legs crossed right over left, shoulders slouched and head cocked to the right. I see myself in her, as she must see herself in me.

I closed my eyes and dreamed of reaching up into the sky to pull down heaven just for her. She deserved every piece of it. When she had started battling cancer, I was too young to understand. Only now do I feel the impact of what was happening. When she was sick, I never felt more hopeless. I wanted to heal her, to help her sleep, to take the pain on myself. And when she cracked her pelvic bone (from which she has yet to heal), I wanted to give her my youth and my strength. But I can only give her my love.

I used to hate to ski. I was too weak, too little, too young. But my mother was determined to share this passion for the slopes with me. Through broken equipment, chilling winds and cold after cold, I grew to understand her zeal for the sport. Skiing is no longer a chore. I've learned to cherish these times that bring us together.

I carry within me her moods and the temper triggered by fatigue. She's often told me exactly what I don't want to hear, not as a mother, but with a stubborn, righteous claim. And I do the same.

"You're only depressing yourself with work!" I say, frustrated because we suffer for it. Yet I often do the same. We fight like sisters, but live for work and play together.

She reaches out to hold my hand as we walk down the hallway. I squeeze it extra hard with a silent "thank you for coming." As we head home, I think about how I truly had fun that night at school.

"Danielle!" she calls hours later with beautiful French pronunciation. "Get off the phone and finish your studying." Her tone rises at the end, as if asking a question, but I hardly notice her accent anymore. She doesn't know that I'm in bed and already off the phone; she's tired. I don't bother to argue. Someday I will move out, and eventually she will move on to a greater life. My biggest wish is that she may influence my children as she did me. I can never thank her enough. 回

I Am a Mother

by Kimberly Blaisdell

I remember the day quite clearly. It was dreary, just like most days in my state. The weather wasn't even half the cause of my gloominess, though. It was the news I received.

I was fifteen years old and dating the bad boy of all time. I was young and stupid. I thought I was invincible to the effects of drugs, sex and pregnancy; boy, was I wrong. After dating for only two months, we broke up, and I found out news that would change my life.

In a room with white walls covered by posters about pregnancy and options, the word came to me as I sat on an overstuffed sofa. A nurse entered, and I handed her a black film container with its lid snapped on tightly. When she opened it, it was not film she exposed, but my fate.

Positive. The word ran through my mind a million times, and dizziness set in. I slouched and forced myself not to cry. I knew my mom would be so upset and that my life would never be the same.

I arrived home, and the weather began to change. But it wasn't the sun making me sweat, it was Mom's questions. I told her the truth, and the screaming began. For seven months we fought. She did everything in her power to make me believe that adoption was the best option for me. I knew she loved me and didn't want me to throw away my life or dreams. So, confused and worn down, I finally gave in. For a month, I searched for the best parents for my unborn son and finally I found them. Two days later, at school, my labor began.

I was in agony for nineteen hours. The contractions hurt, but the fear of losing my son nearly killed me. I knew that while he was inside me, he was mine. Once he was born, I felt like my life would be over.

I held my precious son for the first few seconds of his life, then a nurse gave him to my mom so I could rest. Two hours later, when I awoke, she was still cradling him.

The next day, the adoptive parents came to get him. As they stood outside my room, I broke down as I held my tiny son. I knew then that I should not do this. After hours of crying and begging, my mom agreed. I guess the two hours of bonding did some good.

Here I am today, a seventeen-year-old mother, attending college and working part-time. Every day I face new struggles, but nothing compares to motherhood. My son is almost twenty months old. I wonder sometimes if he would have been better off with a mother and father who could afford to give him more, but not once have I regretted my decision. This is not to say that being a teen parent is easy. I sometimes feel guilty about being selfish and wanting him for myself instead of giving him the chance of a better life. Every day I let him know how much I love him.

If I could go back in time and change some of my choices about drugs, sex and friends, I definitely would.

I would have listened to my mom more, because now I know where she was coming from. Being a teen parent is the hardest challenge I have ever had to face. There is nothing glamorous about waking up every two hours during the night, or rushing your child to the doctor when he has a seizure or another asthma attack. I hate the nights when he's afraid and screams for me, even though I am by his side. I fear the day when I have to tell him where his father is.

I am no longer the same person. I live for my son now, and my success comes from him. I am a mother. ▣

Photo by Caitlin Bird

Too Close

by Alison Riley

A few years ago, my father had a heart attack. I think about it all the time; it has affected so much about my life. I have written this piece in my head a million times.

That spring break, my father and I were vacationing at my grandmother's house far from home. The three of us had planned to go out for dinner, but my father was not feeling well. So, my grandmother and I went without him.

We spent dinner discussing how my grandparents had met, their courtship and engagement. We talked about my grandfather's views on child-rearing, and about his death two years before. He died of too many heartaches, my grandmother said. What I remember is him lying on their couch after so many heart attacks and cursing at how the buttons on his sweater always caught on the crocheted blanket that covered him. He was a wonderful man, we both agreed. I loved how he always noticed little things like buttons in blankets, and she loved his vulnerability under that blanket.

My grandmother asked why I thought my father hadn't come. Even though I was tired of reassuring her that nothing was wrong, I did it once again. He had said he was not feeling well and chose to stay home to rest. She always wanted to make sure no one had a problem or was mad with her and needed to go through a process of checking before settling into a real conversation. I lost patience, as I had seen my father do many times, but felt guilty after I snapped at her. Seeing how hurt she was, I apologized.

On the ride home, her car smelled like the cigarettes she used to smoke and the butterscotch she had replaced them with.

I opened the door even before she stopped the car. I ran in the house, through the kitchen and the family room. My father was there. I thought he was watching TV, lying on the floor, but I had no idea. . . .

"Hi, Dad," I called out.

"Hi, Al," I heard him say.

When I walked back into the family room, my grandmother was quizzing my father. He was in a great deal of pain. She was on the phone, repeating our address for the sixth time. When she put down the receiver, she missed the phone.

She told me to go wait for the ambulance. My head was spinning as I ran outside. I strained my eyes to see the man in the driver's seat of the Honda coming up our driveway. I glanced at the back seat, thinking there was no way my father would fit back there. He assured me that the ambulance was on its way.

From there everything begins to blur together. I clearly remember watching him being helped during the three hours the ambulance sat in front of my grandmother's house. Eventually, it left for the hospital.

I stayed behind at the house. I was afraid of hospitals. Being there would have been too much. I waited for calls from the hospital and talked to people from home. I hated being in North Carolina, so far away from the things that would make me feel better. The plan was for me to stay with neighbors for the night. I grabbed my father's handkerchief as I left. I cried into it all night. It still hangs over the corner of my mirror.

The next morning, I went to the hospital. He had had two more heart attacks that night. But when I saw him, he wanted to know who had won the Red Sox/Yankees game. I cried harder. I would miss him too much.

Days went by, and I was supposed to return to our home. I didn't know if he would recover, but I wanted to be home. Miraculously, he flew home a few weeks later. He was stable, but weak and very scared. I felt five years old giving him a hug, and I felt like he was five years old, too. I found it hard to trust his health or depend on him. I hated to think about him dying.

Things have changed an awful lot between my father and me since the night of his heart attack. No matter how much our relationship continues to evolve or how much distance comes between us, I will always remember each moment of that night because I lived them as if they were his last. ▣

Spaghetti Sauce

Fiction by Brianna Lee

In the vast, clanging whirlpool of Kipling, Mozart, Picasso and Curie, standing in the center with flat red slippers and highlighter-blue eyes, was Mrs. Olivia-Jean Sarber Newcandy, known to me as Ma.

Ma could have climbed Mount Everest without shoes, swum across Lake Michigan with her hands tied behind her back, eaten thirteen boxes of Godiva two-pound assorted chocolates and not gained even a fraction of a pound. She could run a marathon, discover Atlantis, catch a fairy in a jar, find a needle in a haystack, write a novel, end starvation in Africa and still make it home in time for lunch.

But most of all, she could cook.

The food Ma prepared would make you drool at the mere mention: sizzling fish fillets, chicken Parmesan, beef stroganoff . . . even a conventional meatloaf was enough to make the president want to visit our home. She could make meals so delectable that when Julia Child flashed on the television screen, all you could do was laugh.

Spaghetti was an exceptionally fine treat, especially for such a lugubrious Saturday evening as the night I turned seven. Ma was in the kitchen humming the last few bars of "I've Been Working on the Railroad" while taking out the plum tomatoes from the ninety-nine-cent fruit bowl we'd bought at a flea market. Her wooden ladle clattered against the simmering pot as my shriek shattered the air.

"What is it, baby?" she cried, turning away from the stove, expecting to see me with a severed finger or gasping on the floor in wild convulsions.

"I almost reached the Notorious Nelf-Droid, but Xamagag came out of nowhere and attacked me!" I whined, shaking the control pad in frustration. "I was *this* close!" I pinched my fingers together to let her know how thin the distance was between me and the evil Nelf-Droid, nightmare of Belipolya, threat to my kingdom and my most honorable adversary.

"Zamma who?" Ma asked, not doing too good a job of hiding the exasperation on her face as she turned away.

"Xamagag, the Nelf-Droid's evil minion who's actually a good guy, but he got hypnotized and now he thinks that he's the Prince of Belipolya, but really he's just . . ."

"That's nice, sugar," Ma drawled, stirring the cauldron of boiling secrets and hidden miracles within the syrupy tomato mix. "Why don't you put down that game and help me with the spaghetti, huh? Whatdya say, baby?"

"Okay, Ma," I consented, and switched off my player.

"Here now, see this bunch of mushrooms I chopped up? Put them in the big pot right over there." Ma pointed, and, with as much obedience and dignity as I had, I brought the mushrooms to the pot, climbed up on a stool and poured them in. The scarlet solution sizzled and bubbled for a minute before swallowing the handful of spring dreams I'd delivered.

Immensely pleased with my job, I skipped back to the dinner table. Ma stopped me.

"Not so fast, dumplin'," she said. Ma had a voice as smooth as lemon pudding, but at the same time as stinging as a triple slap across the face. "Ain't over yet. I still got a few more things for you to do."

Ma was notorious for her tendency to understate. "Stir the sauce!" she said, and I did. "Pour in those peppers! Get me the meatballs! Pour some of those in, too. Careful not to burn yourself! Keep stirring the sauce—no, no, stir clockwise, Crista, clockwise—didn't anybody ever tell you the other way is bad luck?" Nobody had, of course, but I'd learned long ago that parents like to be right, and it was always best to make them feel good about themselves, so I didn't argue.

The more I poured into the sauce and the more I stirred—clockwise, of course—the higher the steam rose and the more divine it smelled.

Fish of goblin, eye of newt, I chanted to myself while stirring, *liver of codfish, fingers blue . . . which of these will make the stew?* I cocked my eyebrow mysteriously, just like the witches did on the Halloween Channel when they were cooking up something insidiously delightful to serve to the King of Spain just to watch him writhe.

The heavenly perfume fully attacked my nostrils, entering through my ears and mouth and filling my head. The shimmering steam was all around me now, whispering, "Taste me, somebody, taste me," in a way that was as tempting as a newly unwrapped grape lollipop.

How was I to resist? I couldn't stand another minute without a taste! Just one fingerful would do—just one dipped finger and my desires would all be curbed, my wishes all fulfilled.

Before my conscience had time to step in on my thoughts (that conscience was awfully tricky—you had to act quickly before it ruined everything), my finger had dug a small tunnel in the concoction.

"Oh!" I almost cried. The heat sent shocking sensations up my hand. Ma was behind me, rummaging in the cupboard for a pack of noodles, singing, "Someone's in the kitchen with Di-nah, someone's in the kitchen I kno-o-o-ow." Determined not to let a suspicious detail loose, I kept my lips tightly closed, my agonized cry muffled and sounding more like, "Omrhmf!" I twisted my head back in fear; Ma hadn't flinched.

I split my lips apart and stuck the damaged finger in my mouth, letting the soft tomato goodness roll over my tongue. Oh, rapture! Heavenly taste of tastes! The essence of it all . . . that moment was purely indelible. I was dancing on air! I was waltzing on a cloud, skipping into the sunshine!

And . . . I craved more.

No, no, a fingerful wouldn't do this time; it most certainly would not! I wanted to fill the ladle with heaps of sauce, mounds of it! Just one, insignificant, minuscule ladle—oh, perhaps two—and I would never ask for anything again.

I lifted the wooden spoon, filled with hot, steaming joy, and brought it to my lips, tipping the savory contents down my throat. I had hardly gasped for air when a second ladle was brought to my mouth, another mouthful of sauce sent spilling down my tongue.

I was erupting in spaghetti sauce delight. The flavor! The indescribable, unbelievable, supernatural taste! I had to have more!

"Crista!"

I whirled around, half-filled ladle in hand, thin traces of tomato sauce trickling down the sides of my mouth.

"What on God's green earth are you doing?"

I blinked. "I—I'm testing the sauce for you, Ma," I replied, trying to muster a sweet smile I knew would look irresistibly adorable accompanied by the tomato smeared across my chin.

The smile failed. "Crista, do you know how many germs you have in your mouth and your hands? You never taste a sauce before it's ready. You've ruined it now; you've ruined my sauce. Get out of the kitchen, Crista."

The grin dropped from my face like eggs spattered onto the floor. Shock filled my innards. Ma had furious creases cut down the sides of her face; her dark brown curls flared out from her scalp. Her hands were plastered on her hips, and the steely blue eyes burned into my flesh with rage. She was . . . she was angry. My throat had gone dry, my mind stripped of things to say.

I gulped and climbed down from the little stool.

"I just wanted a taste," I whispered as I rounded the corner.

Ma went to fix her sauce, no longer singing, and I played my game in the living room. Suddenly, the thought of encountering the Notorious Nelf-Droid didn't seem very exhilarating. I sat in silence until Ma called me for dinner.

I trotted into the kitchen, hands in my pockets, and sullenly accepted the plate. She plopped on a wad of noodles; I liked to pretend they were worms, giving them names before I ate them. Now, however, I just looked at them and sighed.

Ma walked over to the stove and gripped the ladle. She swished the steaming mix for a bit before picking up a spoonful, preparing to spread it over my noodles.

"I won't be having any sauce, Ma," I said quietly.

"What?" Ma looked at me, her eyes blazing, cheeks beginning to flush.

Don't say it, my conscience warned me. *Don't say it— you'll only get into trouble!*

"I won't be having any sauce," I said again.

"You mean you're just going to eat plain noodles and cheese?" Ma asked in an icy tone.

I nodded timidly. Ma had a crazy look on her face, like she was going to hit me with the ladle, or cuss, or else yell at me that there was no logical reason why I wouldn't have any sauce because she spent a fat lot of trouble making it, even without me messing it up, and I didn't appreciate what I was given, and that back in her day she'd always eaten her meals and thanked the Lord for what little her poor starving family could afford.

But Ma simply put the spoon back in the sauce, placed her hands on her hips and stared into the air.

"Well," she said slowly after a while. "That sounds like a mighty fine idea."

I blinked many times and stared wide-eyed as she put

the lid back on the pot and carried her plate of plain
noodles to the dinner table. I followed her, intrigued and
a bit frightened. Mrs. Olivia-Jean Sarber Newcandy, eating spaghetti without the sauce! I'd sooner expected the
apocalypse. Ma took the jar of Parmesan cheese and
sprinkled it on her noodles. She handed me the cheese;
I did the same.

For a nanosecond before we tasted our naked noodles,
my eyes matched hers, green pitted against blue. Hers
smiled, sparkled and gave a tiny mischievous twitch;
mine responded in kind. Our eyes instantaneously fell
back to our plates. As she bit into her first morsel, I
twirled Sammy, Frank and Georgina around my fork.

I was certain of it now: My ma could balance the world
on her shoulders, fly to the moon with paper wings, do
a triple axel without even putting on skates, read *War
and Peace* in less than an hour and make the best
spaghetti sauce in the universe, even if nobody tasted it.

But then, who couldn't taste it? ◙

Art by Yoon Jeong Choe

I Look Like My Mother

by Karen M. Moran

"You look like your mother," people tell me,
tears in their eyes.
Her reddish-brown hair
lies on my shoulders.

"You look so much like your mother," people say.
"Figure and all."
Tiny and petite.
Small fingers.
Short, oval nails.
Skin as white as snow.

"You look exactly like your mother," people tell me,
tears in their eyes.
Long black lashes
and eyes glassy green.
"Thank you," I say and walk away,
tears in my eyes.

Closer

by Sara Clark

My mother and I used to argue, our relationship like a roller coaster for years. Like me, she has a horrible attitude when she doesn't feel like functioning. Sometimes my sister or I would ask her a question, and she would turn around, eyes full of red rage, and say, "What do you want?" I often had to take a step back so all that anger didn't choke me. Of course, she always apologized later and said she didn't mean it; I think sometimes, though, she did.

"You look like a slut, Sara. You're trying to show off way too much," my mother icily explained one morning before school. The outfit she had so affectionately referred to consisted of a pair of high-heeled black shoes, a black miniskirt and a black tank top with an off-white cardigan over it. My outfit wasn't breaking any school dress codes so I didn't see what she was mad about.

"Do girls at your school wear these types of outfits?" My mother drilled me, eyeing my fashion masterpiece with utter disgust. I refused to answer; I didn't pay attention to most of the girls at school. Of course, I had seen some wear things like this, but not many. Instead, I asked her, "I thought you wanted me to be an individual? My outfit is not inappropriate for school, so what's your problem?"

"You know what? Wear whatever you want . . . I don't care anymore. Just don't be surprised when people at school call you a slut," she replied, never bothering to answer my question. Then she stomped off to her room in a huff and slammed the door. I was left wondering if she really did think I was a slut.

So I guess I would consider myself to be Daddy's girl, at least until things got crazy between us. I got along with him about seventy-five percent of the time and used to feel like I could talk to him about anything. We've always had a close relationship, even before I was born. My mom told me that when she was pregnant, I would move to whichever side my dad was on. My father understands me because we are a lot alike, which is why we are having so many problems now. Because I know exactly what to say to make him boil like water on the stove and vice versa, our discussions often turn into shouting and cursing matches.

In spite of this, though, I realized that my dad can read my mind. When I was in first grade, I remember being in school and getting a horrible stomachache. Painfully shy, I was too scared to go to the nurse. Then, Mr. Mosely, the principal (and my salvation at the time), called me down to the office. Curious, I was shocked to find my dad sitting there. With an umbrella in one hand and an overly anxious expression on his face, he looked like a long-haired, hippie version of Mr. Rogers, minus the happy pills.

"Are you okay, honey?" My dad asked me, while studying my face. He continued, "I brought you an umbrella because I didn't want you to walk home in the . . ."

Before he finished his pathetic excuse for an excuse, he saw my eyes fill with tears. I ran to him and cried on his shoulder. Everything was okay; my daddy was here, and he would take care of things. Driving home, I asked him, "How did you know I was sick?"

"I had a feeling, Sara . . . and I went with it," he replied, giving me a special smile.

Unfortunately, my dad and I don't have that kind of relationship anymore, but we can still sense what the other is thinking. Arguing with him is one of the worst things in the world because if I hurt him with my words, then I feel it. It is like bouncing a rubber ball against a wall; it will always come back and smack you in the face. I try not to talk to him and hope that when we've both grown up more, we can have a relationship again.

About a year and a half ago, my dad and mom started having problems. They would scream at each other about money, getting divorced or staying married, the van, the truck, and back to money, slamming doors and breaking things in the process. Then, my dad would pack his clothes and say, "Have a nice life." Even though he did this several times, once was enough for me. Our relationship has not been the same.

Once I had seen him as a hero; now I saw him as my worst enemy. Our arguments intensified, getting louder and crueler each time. Emotions bounced off walls, affecting the mood of the entire household for days. He would cry and say things like, "I have no wife . . . no kids . . . no friends . . . no life" in a pathetic, heart-wrenching attempt to make us all feel sorry for him.

Every time he did that, I left the room; I couldn't stand to see my daddy cry.

While our relationship deteriorated, my mother and I grew closer. I found that I can talk to her now. I understand why my mom acted the way she did, and I'm glad to report that she's really trying to improve her attitude. Despite our problems, my mom and I can manage to have a good time together. We're closer than we've ever been, although she still criticizes my outfits. With real love, you can't make yourself stop caring, no matter how much it hurts. I love my father, and I feel he loves me. I realize that he just doesn't know how to show it. In the end, all we can do is try. 回

I Know You Now

by Laura Robichaux

My mother
She is a mysterious figure in my life;
Lately she comes and goes like the wind.
Although present in some tenses,
She is not.
I feel I barely know her at times.

But she has good intentions,
Which correspond with her warm heart.
For what other reason would she still be willing to argue
* for my causes—*
to stand up to my father, the parent with whom I live.

How else but for these attributes,
These that define her so well,
Could she raise three children. And give up all her time.
To attend plays, recitals, and the practices in between,
the soccer games, the volleyball tournaments, and
* the cheerleading meets.*

She has a pure heart, a forgiving spirit, and a voice
that can soothe the deepest wound, blunt the
* sharpest words.*

And as if this is not enough
console my friends,
when their own moms cannot.

She ate plastic food, and conversed with bears,
She cared for my dolls and wiped their tears
Just as she did with me.
When I am sick
She still brings me soup, just as if I were five,
No meal could compare to hers,
The love that is found in each bite are in
*   her dishes alone.*

I realize now,
I do know you.
Even though we may drift apart, from time to time.
You are unchanging, my reliable constant,
You maintain the balance in my life.

Mom,
my irreplaceable companion,
Forgive me, please, I am afraid I know you
Better than I thought.
I am grateful for this calm.
But when will the winds shift again?

Whose Child?

by Elizabeth Torpey

arolyn had this enormous, oak-framed sofa in her office. It was long and bizarre with stiff, square, violet and gold-streaked cushions, squatting low and ominously. It matched nothing in the room, but at the same time had a confident presence. When I sat in it, I felt small and awkward because at five foot one, my legs dangled over the side with no hope of ever reaching the floor, but somehow this gave me a sense of safety. It always took me almost the entire session to get comfortable, and today was no exception I realized, as I glanced with heavy eyelids at the digital clock on Carolyn's disorganized desk behind her.

She was smoothing her billowy silk skirt over her knees. It was floor-length, made of some wildly exotic African design in shining coppers and browns and rusty oranges. Her wardrobe sometimes amazed me.

"You have really rotten self-esteem, Liz," she said matter-of-factly. "You're pretty; you're smart; you've got lots of friends . . . and you're a good person. But there's still something inside you that's pulling you down and destroying your inner confidence."

I didn't want to meet her eyes. Of course, everything she was saying was true, because she was my therapist, and she was never wrong. There was a part of me that felt ashamed for thinking such degrading thoughts about myself and being so helpless at trying to stop; the knowledge that so many others had worse problems hovered over my conscience. And I was embarrassed.

"I really believe," Carolyn declared, "that people who are adopted have a built-in insecurity about themselves. They have a fear of rejection right from the beginning— after all, their biological parents have given them away, and they immediately start to think, *What's wrong with me? Why wasn't I kept? Wasn't I good enough?*" She paused and smiled at me sympathetically with her coral painted lips. "Face it, Liz, it comes with the territory. There's no way to avoid it. And it's not your fault."

I always felt rather strange when she brought up my adoption as the reason for things. It was like suddenly being plucked from the present, out of my terrible, familiar, normal teenage life, and being whizzed back to that early, early part of my childhood that from the very beginning had made me different. It all felt so complicated, but it made sense, too.

I was holding Carolyn's unwavering gaze now, not wanting to speak because I knew she was on the absolute verge of saying something important.

"I've been thinking about this for the past week or so, since our last session." She shifted gracefully in her chair. "And I'm wondering if it's about time for you to start thinking about searching for your birth parents."

I know that my facial expression hardly changed, but the nerves in my stomach began to jerk and shake, and my heart started to punch against my ribs, and this sensation of tingling and utter confusion spread through my body.

I nodded understandingly.

"Maybe meeting with them and talking to them about why they put you up for adoption would help. . . ."

I moistened my lips, which had become dry and stiff. "I know consciously why they did it."

She bobbed her head vigorously in reply. "Of course you do. And you have dealt with it all very well. But there's a part of you that doesn't know, that isn't satisfied. Maybe you would feel more secure and resolved, and somehow better about yourself, if you could fill in what you don't know about your life and the people who brought you into this world." She was quiet for a moment. "Liz, you think about it for a while. If you're not comfortable with the possibility, then that's absolutely fine. But if you feel it would help you to learn more about yourself, then we'll do what we can to reunite you with your birth parents."

All I could do was continue to nod. What could I say? I felt different, detached, and in a way, alone, like nobody's child.

I left Carolyn's office that day feeling lost. ▣

Nameless

by Nicholas Taylor

I have a somebody. a nobody. an idea. an epiphany.
A concept of fatherhood abruptly shattered.
This someone. this person. this symbol of broken love.
shall remain nameless. here. now and forever.
Nameless now. nameless then. all my fears
    will rise again.
Yet nameless is what he remains. human qualities
    he cannot attain.
My loves. my pleasures. my walls and bridges.
are dampened. and bleak. because of his absence.
    his flight.
My best days are my worst days. all my days remain
    the same
dark and bleak. forgotten and depressed.
days of hell where joy is suppressed.
So Nameless here, now and forever.
he presses against my soul.
I feel it now. I've felt it before.
The drippings of my soul. secreted to the floor.
into a lonely puddle. a puddle of tears.
where no fatherly hand has touched in years.
So soon the tears will wash away.
the circumstances of another day.

the circumstances of another day.

In Dreams

Fiction by Danielle Lukowski

The sun glittered in a shade of yellow I never knew existed. Along with the trees and greenish-blue shimmer of the lake, the whole scene reminded me of some Grateful Dead T-shirt wrapped around our boat. It was so incandescently beautiful I almost forgot the purpose of today's vacation. I reluctantly reached for my fishing pole, plotting ways not to touch the bait we had selected earlier that morning when the sky showed no promise of becoming this impressive. It made me want to write poetry. I do not write poetry.

"What do you think heaven looks like?"

My father looked up from my fishing pole, which he had begun hooking, and pondered my question.

"I think heaven looks exactly like this: my boat surrounded by a couple hundred yards of lake on each side. My pole in hand and the sun on my face, only my dad would be sitting here with me. I haven't gone fishing with my father for almost thirty years. That's what heaven will be like. For me."

Wow. Now I had to start thinking, because I knew he would ask me in return. To me, heaven seemed like a big lounge where we got to enjoy our lives at whatever age we wanted. It would be a place where we could get those extra hours at the party that ended too soon, where that birthday we could never forget went on for twenty-four days instead of twenty-four hours. But that answer seemed vague and impersonal compared to my father's. It made me feel boring. I hoped he wouldn't ask me.

"What will heaven be like for you?" he asked.

I'm sure he could see my disgruntled expression, even though I pulled every muscle in my face to restrain it.

"Oh, Daddy, I don't know."

"Well, why did you ask me?" He suddenly seemed really interested in what I had to say.

I shrugged. That was the most honest thing I had said yet. I seriously didn't know. Why did I ask him that? I was only seventeen, had no terminal illness and had lost only one close relative. My father had the same profile. The topic of the afterlife had never come up.

"Okay, my turn," my father interrupted my thoughts, which I actually appreciated. I was anxious to hear his question, though. He was rendering me speechless with his interest in this topic.

"Do you look forward to heaven?"

"Yeah," I said. "I really do. I mean, I am not afraid of heaven, because it's supposed to be greater than even the best life on Earth—and eternal. And there is no pain or suffering—but still, just the thought of—just knowing—"

"You're afraid of death."

"No, that's not it at all . . ." I trailed off, trying to defend my point, but it was exactly that. Although I'd never said it, I was a little scared of dying. Okay, I was terrified. I was terrified of leaving everything I knew. I was terrified of living without my family and friends. And most of all, I was terrified of what that meant. My father put his hand on my shoulder, as if he knew how I felt. I knew he didn't; at that moment he did not feel the way I did.

"You don't have to be afraid. I know it's hard, but that's what my dad told me, and I didn't believe him until he was gone. I hope it doesn't take you that long."

Any other person would have been shocked by his last statement, but I knew he was being humorous. And I appreciated it. If I said I believed him I'd be lying, so instead I rested my hand on his and simply smiled. He knew what it meant, too, but instead of looking disappointed, he seemed almost content.

"Are you looking forward to it?" I asked.

My father gazed at the lake for a moment. He cocked his head and did some kind of diagonal nod. At this point all my fears and uncertainties dissolved into tears that welled up in my eyes. A combination of the sun's reflection over the shimmering lake and my father's gaze forced me to look down, gravity pulling my tears toward my already fidgeting feet. My father was less afraid to die than I was of his death. I blinked hard, took several deep breaths and finally summoned my voice.

"Why?"

At this point, all efforts to suppress my crying were lost—lost in the anticipation of his answer and the confusion of my own cowardly response. Tears streamed down my face, flowing over every curve of my cheeks, nose and chin. My father set down his fishing pole and

Art by Audrey Rutledge

hugged me. He held on for a good five minutes before he finally said, "Yes, and no."

I was confused. I glanced up, my eyes weary.

"I don't want to leave you or my wife behind. That's why I used to be afraid. But to fish with my father again, never to lose anyone again and to see you all when you finally join me? I could definitely stand those years by myself if I knew I'd get to spend eternity with the ones I love. So please try to understand that if you lose me, if you lose anyone, it's only a momentary loss. And it'll make it even greater when you get to heaven and see those you've lost in life."

I kissed him on the cheek and rested my head on his chest. It had been more than a while since I'd discussed such insecurity. In fact, it had been never.

"Thank you, Dad."

He patted my head softly and asked, "So—what do you think heaven is like?"

I sighed and closed my eyes, shutting out the daylight. Opening them, I found myself in the dark, staring at my ceiling. Bewildered, I sat up and looked to my left where my husband lay asleep. I wondered what he'd say about a dream this bizarre. But instead of waking him, I slid back under the sheets again. I was actually comforted; it took me ten years, but finally, at 3:27 that morning, for the first time, I truly accepted my father's death. Not as a loss, and not as an ending. Someday I will tell him, when we go fishing once again on that beautiful lake, on that warm summer day. That's what heaven will be like. For me. ▣

Passports:
Finding New Places

Photo by Alexa Schuler

Burned

by Jamie Burklund

I really want to go home," I whisper to my mother.

I'm fifteen years old, sitting in a restaurant booth about to meet my father for the first time. With my back to the door, I can't stop moving. I wonder what he'll look like, what he'll say. My mother asks if I'm nervous. "No," I lie.

I wish I could be anywhere but here. I feel ill every time I hear the door open. It's too early, and I begin to yearn for the comfort of my bed. I try to focus on the conversations around me, but nothing works. I can't stop thinking about what is about to happen. He's late. The thought that he might not come crosses my mind. I tell myself that he probably forgot. My thoughts comfort me, but not for long.

"There he is. He's walking in right now," my mother tells me. She forces a smile. I want to disappear. I turn to see my father—a stranger. We make eye contact. He is my height, blond, with blue eyes and bronzed skin. I smile, but feel like throwing up. He sits across from me, but talks to my mom before speaking to me.

"Hey, Babe," he finally says to me. He has a Southern

accent, and I wonder where he picked that up. As far as I know, he's always lived in Michigan.

Now it's my turn to force a smile. I can't look at him, and his calling me Babe makes me want to spit in his face.

He stares at me for a few minutes. The waitress comes and I feel like thanking her. She quickly takes our orders and leaves. I want to cry.

My father turns to me again. I act like I don't realize he's staring. I don't want to look at him, not even once, but I finally do. We both have blond hair. That's it. I don't look anything like him, but I have no doubt he's my father.

He begins a conversation with my mother. I realize I act like him and wonder how that's possible. I can tell by looking at him that he is nervous, too. I can't help thinking that I want this to be over. I'm shaking because I know I'm going to have to talk to him and really don't want to. I want to be home, sleeping.

I listen to his voice and force back tears. *This is my father,* I think. I wonder why he has never wanted to be a part of my life until now. For a second I want to hug him and tell him I love him. But I don't—I know I'd regret that later. I tell myself I hate him and couldn't care less if I ever see him again. I know that's not true, either.

Now my father has turned his attention to me. He tells me I'm pretty, asks about boys, school. I answer in short sentences and nod.

We leave the restaurant and make plans to meet at our apartment. He doesn't remember how to get there, so he follows us. At home, he tells me how sorry he is for never being around. He says he wants to be part of my life now and will try his hardest to be a good dad. He makes many promises, and finally gives me a hug and leaves.

I haven't seen my father since, and the restaurant where we met burned to the ground. ▣

Photo by Connor Kelley

Sara on the Wall

Fiction by Brett Elizabeth Larkin

I sit at our kitchen table thoughtfully munching a bagel, slouching in the dark.

"It is a total dump down here," my sister Sara says, pulling the chain above my head to turn on the light. My eyes shudder at the sudden brightness even though I have been up for an hour and am ready for school. I look up at her, the light on her scalp reflecting the many hair colors she has had in the past two years.

"What?" she asks, towering over me. I feel so small and helpless as I sit, she so luminous in her platform shoes.

"You driving?" I ask dully.

"No, Kirk Gallenger is giving me a ride. Looks like it's the bus for you," she says, twisting her shirt around so it reveals part of her stomach. "Tell Mom I left. If she even gets up today."

"Get lost," I say. "Is Kirk boyfriend-of-the-week?" She uses my breakfast plate as an ashtray in response.

"Don't do that," I say, miserably.

"Go to hell," she says, throwing the rest of her cigarette out the window. It misses and falls to the floor where other junk is lying around. Sara does not notice, and I hear her slam the front door behind her.

I slowly get up to follow. Reaching into my pocket, I

make sure the switchblade I stole from our neighbor's garage is still there. When Freddie Cooger and his gang come after me today, I will be ready.

My school is so big I always feel helplessly lost. There are at least 250 sophomores, and you can lose your identity in the swarming mass of students. The school's front doors, walls and floors are mocha brown. I hate mocha brown, but it represents the school perfectly, and it is also the color of the vanilla yogurt from the machine in the cafeteria.

With my first step in the door, my hand zooms to my pocket, making sure the knife is still there. I have to be ready, defensive and quick, like Jackie Chan in *Rumble in the Bronx*.

I go to science first block. We are doing an experiment with phenol red today that might be worthwhile. Sam Freemor, Jack Renalds, Kraig Skyler and I skip math, though; I hate math, it's such a waste of time. Next is Spanish, and only Beth Harrison and I show up because there is a test. Spanish tests are okay because I am pretty much fluent; my dad spoke Spanish with me when I was little and it sort of stuck. I decide to take the dumb thing. I don't have anything better to do.

Lunch rolls around and I sit alone. Eventually, Bud Herrup sits down next to me.

"What's up?" he asks.

"Nothing," I say. My sister is standing at a table in front of me with her arms around Derek Holson, the quarterback, who is more than three times my size. The thought of him makes me put my hand in my pocket again. The knife is still there; today I am sick of being pushed around.

Dan Turner, a junior, comes over and puts his arm around me.

"Hey, when are you going to hook me up with your sister, Dude?" he asks, staring at Sara.

"I was wondering the same thing," says Bud, laughing.

"Get lost," I tell Dan, staring through the busy cafeteria at my sister.

"Defending her, huh?" Dan asks, laughing.

"No, just get over it," I tell him. My sister and I have no relationship whatsoever. It's just like she happens to live in the same house. No childhood memories. I do not know her and don't even want to.

I see Cindy Lipman, a junior, through the bustling cafeteria. She was voted student president last year and still assumes the position since no election was set up this year. She's wearing jeans and a white turtleneck, has a perfect pale complexion and light pink lips. Her wavy blonde hair bounces as she sits with her giddy friends. My sister is just as well known around the school as Cindy, but they are nothing alike.

"Hey Rick, you going to English? We have that test, you know," Bud says to me. Dan has left.

"Yeah, I'll be there," I say, still looking straight ahead. English is the only class I like.

"You'll ace it, you know," Bud says, annoyed. Kids always get annoyed because I ace tests. I don't study, just kill the tests, that's how I do it. I pick up a textbook once in a while, which is more than most kids, but I only do it on a strictly need-to-know basis.

I see Freddy Cooger and his friends eating and quickly get up, throwing away my food. I reach into my pocket and feel the knife against my leg as I walk quickly out of the cafeteria. I enter the boys' bathroom and lean against the graffiti-covered wall, feeling safe. My heart starts beating normally again and I turn around. Where my head was resting is my sister's name, with all sorts of horrible swears and curses around it, scratched in the wall. I am sure I've seen this before, but it never really caught my attention.

"Sara," I whisper, blowing away the dust and dirt from where her name is scratched, tracing the outline of the letters with my finger. I bring my hand up, cleaning her name with my sleeve, then draw my knife, switching the sharp blade out for the first time. I hear the bell ringing for English, yet I stay in the bathroom scratching away the curses, the name-calling and the taunts. Slowly, my knife cuts away at the painful words, disintegrating them into a pile of dust on the bathroom tile at my feet.

In less than forty minutes I am done, leaving only her name, Sara, pure, simple and fresh, the way it should be. I pause a moment to admire my work, then kick the pile of dust, throw my knife in a trash can and leave to catch the last few minutes of class. 回

Wither

by Pam Smykal

Mint green leather chairs. Dull mint green, the material was split from use and the stuffing was pouring out. I sat on this chair, watching my grandfather wither away. At first, we discussed anything that came to mind; now all was silent. Awkward silence. He was still awake, I knew, just staring straight, with no television on. He didn't speak much these days. Once again he was admitted to the hospital, the second time in two months. The problems kept coming, his health suffering, and his attitude toward life was deteriorating. How much more could words say? I knew my regrets weren't going to fix the damage from the stroke or the confused stare he gave as I walked through the doorway. Too many things had hit him at once, and he decided not to fix any of it. This prolonged visit was due to an infection in his feet, and once again, something wasn't getting better.

"Do they hurt?" I asked from the sustained silence.

"Huh?" He looked at me with his eyes glazed over, hair combed to one side. He seemed to droop. The comparison to a wilting flower was inevitable. His skin took on a rubbery texture and was gray.

"Do your feet hurt? Are you okay?" I stumbled . . .

trying, trying to regain composure. Of course they probably hurt; the infection was in both of his feet, which my parents had described as feeling like they were dying. Nobody dared to ask what would be next.

My grandfather didn't answer right away, which was normal. He just sat there, looking wistful as if suddenly tomorrow he'd wake up and become young again, and would actually smile.

"No, I'm fine for now." Each word was pronounced separately. I was at a loss for everything. Nothing to focus on. Even the weather was dreary, and I still had a forty-five-minute drive back, though I wouldn't cut this short.

"I haven't seen you in awhile; you're looking pretty good," I lied. The last hospitalization had left him forty pounds lighter, with fluid movements that made him appear as if he was treading water with difficulty.

"I haven't been feeling too well. Everything hurts. The food is terrible. It could be worse," he finished with a chuckle. I smiled; he was trying.

"Was it bad coming here?" he asked.

I drove down to surprise him with my newly earned license. I didn't want him to think my parents forced me into this visit either, because they hadn't. I just knew I had to see him, because he was always depressed if my brothers and I were not able to visit.

"No, no. The roads are fine. Not much snow." I was a terrible talker. My mother was always the one to keep a conversation going, even with my grandfather. I was more of a thinker. Words did not tumble out as easily as they filtered through my head. I was even known for "thinking too much." Perhaps it was my escape. My grandfather laid back again, trying to relax, looking stiff. I knew this was a sign that it was time to leave. I scolded myself for not being comforting enough, not being open or talkative. No wonder he wanted to be alone; I wasn't much company.

"I'm sorry," I started to apologize.

"I don't need an apology. Nothing is your fault. Thank you. Thank you for being here, for trying," my grandfather slowly closed his eyes.

I smiled, kissed him on the cheek and walked out. ◙

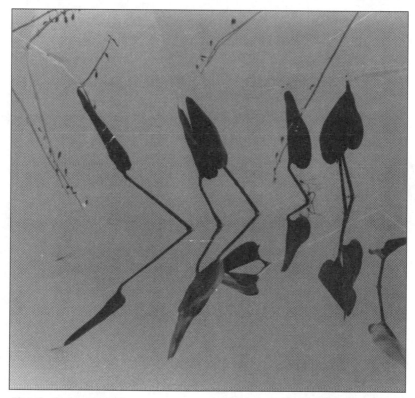

Photo by Stephen Siperstein

Sparkill Cemetery

by Sarah Davis

Through the deserted graveyard
We drove
Winding our way through
Hairpin curves
Radio blaring.
We were looking for Dan,
Acting like Dan,
But sober.
He would laugh,
But we did not laugh
We never did find Dan
Maybe he did not wish
For our tears to fall
For him
So Dan, and the stone that marked
His newfound home,
Played hide-and-seek with us,
And won.

The Missing Piece

by Nathan V. Koch

My life is like a puzzle. I have edge pieces that enclose the inner ones, the funny-looking jigsaw pieces with five or six knobs apiece, and the corners that limit its sprawl. But as I grow, pieces of my puzzle come and go. Sometimes I am missing an edge piece and feel melancholy. Or maybe two pieces fit together exactly, and then I am out of sorts and full of anger. When my sister left home for college last August, the center piece of my puzzle was gone.

In a way, I left first. I went to camp the Sunday before her departure, as I had in previous years. I'd always said good-bye before I left, but this time my good-bye would have to last. Even so, her hug wasn't any stronger or her smile any warmer. Amanda and I parted as if we would see each other in a week.

Of course, she wasn't home when I returned. She was many miles away in her new room at school. It didn't register that she was really gone because I never made a "final good-bye" like my parents had when they got in the car to drive home without her.

To tell you the truth, I don't even know when it occurred to me that Amanda wasn't living at home anymore. I think her absence made itself felt in an accumulation of many smaller absences: hearing songs we both loved on the radio, making fun of my parents all by myself and not having to plead with her for my turn on the phone.

All I remember is that I despised the sight of her empty room. I still do. Even though her room has her dressers, bed and bookshelves, it lacks her personality. The smell of her peach spray and girly cosmetics has escaped through the cracks in the windows. Yes, the room is still there, but there is no sign of Amanda.

I tried to keep her door closed the first few weeks, which made it feel as though she were inside, still changing her outfit for the 800th time or taking a nap. The first week of school, I didn't even play my radio in the morning as I got ready, because I still felt like she were in there sleeping, and I didn't want to wake her.

On the other hand, her departure did bring some welcome benefits. The phone was now mine to use at my leisure. I could play video games whenever I wanted, and I wasn't forced to watch *Felicity* every Wednesday night when all I wanted to do was watch *Celebrity Deathmatch*.

But the funniest part was that I started to watch *Felicity* after she left. I actually used the phone less, even though I had it to myself. Even the perks of her departure came to seem less special. There was really nothing good for me about Amanda leaving our cozy house, but I tried to steer away from being selfish by reminding myself that Amanda was becoming an independent woman.

Our initial conversation was after my first day of high school. She asked about my teachers, my friends and, of course, about how annoying Mom and Dad were. We laughed most of the conversation, as we usually did. When we finally prepared to hang up, I blanked. Normally I would say, "See ya later, Amanda." It was different now. We both paused, speechless. Finally, she broke the silence. "I love you, bro. Call me anytime you want."

My mom always said, "People are irreplaceable." I used to just nod, but she is right—there's no substitute for my sister.

I've never told her that I watch *Felicity* since she's gone, though. I don't think I will. It isn't about TV shows. It's about being a brother and sister, and becoming closer than ever before. ◙

Photo by Tiffany Turner

I Remember

by Lisa Miles

I remember when my dad was sick, when his skin turned an unnatural, sallow color and he went to the doctors to see what was wrong.

"It could be a couple of things," they explained. "There's a chance it might be cancer. We're going to have to run more tests." Why does human nature always force us to fear the worst when things might go the other way? I suppose it would be a cruel trick of the mind always to believe the best, but without hope, what is the point?

I remember the day the test results came back. I knew they were coming, but I stayed anyway. I didn't want just to sit all day and wait to find out, as if the waiting and worrying would ensure better results. A call came at my friend's house—*come home.* The trip home was never as long as it was that day. I had nothing to do but pedal and think. I parked and could see my oldest brother through the sliding-glass door waiting for me. He was pacing the dining-room floor, which told me more than words. We didn't say anything, just hugged each other as tightly as we could and cried. He must have squeezed all the tears out of me, because I never cried so much, before or since. From there we went to the hospital to visit our dad.

Six months to live—tops. It is awful to tell a man when he will die. That is something I believe we are not meant to know. Dad told the doctor he would send him a letter in six months—and one day.

The next few months were almost normal. We went camping, fishing, rappelling, jet skiing, all a little more than usual, but not a lot. Then Dad started getting sick again.

I remember sitting at recess one day, clutching our picture in my hand and trying hard not to cry. It was the only picture I had of him and me, taken at a daddy-daughter activity. He was making a fake serious face, wearing a tiny red cowboy hat and a bandanna around his neck. He had his arm around me. It felt as though he were already gone, although I knew he was lying in bed at home, still alive—for the moment. Everyone knew. I hated that everyone knew.

I remember when my dad was dying. I remember the awful smell that permeated his part of the house. I remember the air freshener that none of us can stand to this day because it brings back the horrible memory. "Summer Breeze." How ironic.

I remember him before the cancer, so full of vitality. His sense of humor—everyone loved his sense of humor. I remember the beginning, or rather, the beginning of the end. I remember his skin turning yellow again. I remember him lying in bed, all control of his body and mind slipping away, striving to hold on. I remember a client coming to see him. He tried to get up, babbling, "Gotta draw some lines. Gotta draw some lines." I remember my aunt, his sister, whom I had never been very close to,

holding me in her arms as we sat on the floor of the bedroom, crying.

I remember crying a lot. I cried more before he died
than after. I think we all did. A wife and eight children,
one already gone. He would soon be with that one
again. I remember Rachel singing his favorite hymn,
"How Great Thou Art."

I remember the phone ringing, and for minutes that
seemed like hours, him mumbling, "Hello? Hello? Hello?"
I ran to the living room and threw myself on the couch,
buried my head in pillows, wishing I could sink into the
couch and disappear. I hated to see him like that. It tortured me to hear nonsense coming from him. He was
such an intelligent man, rich with talents, but his mind
was gone. I couldn't take it anymore—I pleaded with
God to free him, to take him home.

It was a relief when he finally passed on. But, although
I knew this was best, the finality was hard to endure. He
was physically gone, I could no longer see him and hope
beyond all hope that his wits would return and he would
recover. He would not.

Over the years I have adjusted. We all have. Our lives
have gone on. I wish he were here. Sometimes I do
things I know he would be proud of. I want to see him
smile and tell me how wonderful they are, and then, very
gently and carefully, tell me that I could do better, not
because it wasn't enough for him, but because he knew
I could. Sometimes I feel his smile and the warmth it
gives my heart. And that is enough for now. ▣

¡Está Bien!

by Lisa Avila

Damn, Lisa! Why you gotta be such a scaredy cat? You sure you a true Chicana?" my friend Consuelo asked, standing right in front of my face and daring me with her eyes. She wanted me to join her and some friends to beat up two girls who were coming toward us. There was no way I was going to get into a fight with those girls. I didn't even know them!

My friend and I are considered Chicanas, which means we are half Mexican and half American. We speak Spanglish when we're together, which means we use both languages, switching when we have no idea how to say something in one. We speak like Mexican gangsters. People think that if you speak like that, you are a gangster. For us it's different, because, of course, we aren't.

My friend, Consuelo Rodriguez, is short, with short black hair and light skin. She came to the United States long before I did. You're probably getting confused. We were born here, but our parents sent us back to Mexico. Consuelo's parents brought her back four years later, but I didn't return until I was fourteen. I didn't know her until I got here. I always make fun of her long name, and of course she gets ticked off, but she laughs, too. She calls me Lisa.

You might say Consuelo is a "hard-core girl," but she isn't. She gets into fights, which sometimes aren't her fault, like what happened about a year ago. Thank God it was the last time. She wanted to beat up those girls, or *morras,* as she calls them. (It is a bad word.) Actually, it depends on the way you use it; if you're talking about your friend, it just means "girl."

That day we were headed to the park with some friends, just to hang out. As we walked, Consuelo made fun of me and how I talk. She says I'm a schoolgirl. The thing is, I do talk like she does, only not as much. My English vocabulary is better than hers, and I know how to spell much better, too. I don't feel like a geek or anything, but it does tick me off when she starts teasing me about the way I talk.

She kept on so I told her to stop. "Would you quit whining? Keep doing that, and I'm going to make you feel sorry." By now I had moved to block her way. My hands were in my pockets, but loose so that if she tried anything I would be able to throw a punch. To my surprise she just stared past me. She had a face that looked so angry, it made me feel sorry I had yelled at her. "What are you looking at, *morra?* You look as if you saw the devil," I said. Turning around, I raised one eyebrow as high as I could.

They were coming, the worst enemies of Consuelo. There were three of them. I knew them; they were in my class. They never, ever spoke a single word, and they didn't bother me at all, either. Consuelo didn't even know their names, but she did know they hated her guts, and all because one of them used to get all the attention from guys, until Consuelo took that away.

"Hey, Lisa?" she asked with her hands formed in fists. "You and those *morras* are in the same class, right?" I didn't answer quickly.

"So what?" I asked, hoping she'd tell me what she was planning.

"C'mon, Lisa, you're the one who never cuts class; you should've figured it out already." She was laughing but still looking forward. Those girls were only a block away now.

"Yeah, I know, but you, you are unpredictable. You make me think you are about to do something, and you end up doing something else!" I said, pushing her away. She had taken me as her target of mocking today. It had been going on since she picked me up at my house.

"That means you at least know their names," she told me as she shoved me aside.

"Yes, I know their names, but they don't talk to me," I answered. I was looking at her back and wishing she wasn't my friend so that I could at least throw a punch, pull her hair or push her into a puddle.

"So, why are you just standing there? Tell me!" she screamed. I was startled. I felt my heart jump.

"Hey, stupid, you didn't have to scream! I'm not deaf, you know," I told her, holding my hips and stretching my neck as far as I could.

"*¡Está bien!*" (okay) she said in a much lower voice.

"The girl with the red jacket, high heels and big hair is Marisela. The one in the middle with the black jacket and black jeans is Araceli. The one all in pink is Rebecca," I told her. She just stood quietly.

Then out of nowhere, she said, "You know, maybe the only way those *morras* are going to keep their mouths shut is if they get a little bit of how it feels to get beat up. They don't know who they're messing with." She was determined to show them she wasn't going to let them push her around. Then she and our other two friends started walking toward them. I stayed behind.

"Lisa, ain't you coming?" she asked, turning around.

"No, I've got no beef with them," I answered, then turned and started walking away.

"You are so pathetic. What kind of friend are you? We are supposed to stand together in times of need," she yelled, making the sign of "I love you" in sign language, only it was upside-down. I had already stopped walking.

"Why is it that it always has to be your·way, huh? Can't you at least try to understand the fact that I'm not like you? I don't just fight 'cause they're talking about me or 'cause I hate them!" I yelled like I had never yelled before. The three girls were listening and mumbling to each other. Consuelo stood frozen. "I guess I never thought you were this upset. I'm sorry I mocked you. But it does tick me off that you don't want to help," she said quietly, though I could hear her clearly.

If we were in Mexico we wouldn't be arguing about whether or not to beat up a girl or two. In Mexico people are more united, at least teenagers. There are gangs there, but not as violent as here in America. The three girls had already walked away.

"I didn't mean to embarrass you in front of them, but you have changed. I don't even know why," I said, as I stood about six steps from her with my shoulders down. I was tired, but it felt good to tell her how I felt.

"Look, I consider you my best friend, but I'm tired of

seeing you so nice, so patient," she said as she looked me straight in the eye. "I'm different from you. I'm more like this messed-up girl. Everybody thinks that I got no feelings, except you; you were my first real friend. Not just looking to me for protection." She had started crying. Her other friends had walked away. It was better that they had left.

I knew why she was the way she was. Mexico was everything for her. She felt free. There, no one tells you you can't climb a tree or run around the streets 'cause you'll get hit by a car. Don't get me wrong; I miss all that, too. But I have my mother and my sister and brother. Consuelo's mom died a while ago during a visit to Mexico. The worst part is that Consuelo and her mom had a fight the day before her mom left. Consuelo says she felt the urge to ask her mom not go to Mexico; I guess she had a feeling something bad was going to happen. I admire Consuelo for being this strong. She has a kind heart, but doesn't want pity from anyone, so she feels the need to show she is not hurt.

After our fight, Consuelo started to change. Now she is different; she's even doing better in school than I am. "I always knew you were the real schoolgirl," I told her recently. Giggling, she said she had to hang up because she hadn't finished her homework. ▣

Crashing over the Edge

by Annie Gaughen

A few years ago, I sat at my desk, my hands grasped my head, tears flowing. One of many times. Tears of loss and confusion ran down my wrist, feeling as cold as metal. Why did I always think these things would never happen to me, never pierce my protective shell? To top it off, I did not have them—the ones I loved and needed. Jane, Nacie, and most important, Becky. My friends. My mainstays. Tomorrow I would not wake at seven-thirty and leisurely hop into the car forty minutes later, happy, well-rested and utterly content if only because I would see my friends ten minutes later.

Instead I would rush out to catch a grumpy bus and dread the brief ride. My breakfast—an apple. Then I would trudge down the rubber-coated steps of the decaying bus, entering this place of misery, masked with bright faces and cheery hellos. This place where concrete walls surrounded you and scraped you, with peeling paint flaking off, as if to remind you that nothing accomplished here was worthwhile enough to last. Where giggling twits in four-inch electric green platforms flounced their big hair and snapped their gum. I would smirk inwardly at their pathetic behavior. But then my smugness would be swallowed in the grievous truth that they had their friends inches away, while mine were miles from here. Then all I could do was to grit my teeth, close my eyes, bite my lip and walk past them to first period.

I hated it. I despised it. I was proud that I was not like them. I was proud that I had higher expectations of the people I hang out with. The expectations I had when I met them. Especially Becky.

Becky is my best friend. She is a wonderful person, but so complex that you have to love her to tolerate her. She's like me. And she always tolerated me. Always.

It was true. Through all my beautiful triumphs and horrible slumps, she was there to whisper encouragement in my ear and grasp me close like some Asian angel. Even when I was a jerk, she stood by me. Even when I sobbed, she stood by me. Even when I was cold toward her, she stood by me. She held my hand and held me up. She was a glimpse of heaven; but now I lived in an earthly replica of hell. Maybe I made it that way myself. I honestly do not know. But I do know that I hated it with such a passion that I had to either kill someone or die.

I chose to die.

Each day I would cry many times, always alone, holed up in a sickeningly barren room, cluttered with meaningless junk. And I would sob until my hands were puckered from moisture. Sometimes my tears were not even shed physically; I felt them sliding down my soul. I let no one know. My mother had her own problems. My older brother did not deal with emotions well. My younger brother would not understand. My father was . . . I don't know. Removed. My friends had always relied on me to be strong, to know the answer to every problem with wonderful and perfect advice. They liked me superhuman.

So there I was. I was standing at the top of a waterfall, grasping the breaking branch. I could not yet understand how far I could plummet. But I knew that any minute I would become part of the icy water.

My grandparents' deaths cemented the deal. They flung an axe directly at the branch, chopped it so that I fell in. Fell into the rush that would throw me, freezing in its arms, over the formidable edge and crashing gladly into death.

I sat awake many nights, alone and totally terrified of myself. Sometimes I would throw open the window, feel the glorious gust of ice pushing through the metal screening, my cage. Snow was on its back. So what would happen if I ran outside to sleep in the darkness and be blanketed in thousands of tiny ice crystals, covering my slowly freezing body? Would it be wonderful to taste my release? My mind flashed to Becky, sobbing and crying at my wake, looking desolate and blank. I would close the window.

One evening Becky was fiddling with my computer, searching through my files while I was in the bathroom. I came back to hear an "Annie?" Her voice sounded devastated, a little weak. There was a shimmer of something in my own mind, something hopeful. I looked at the screen.

My good-bye letter.

It all came out that night. I did not think, at the time, that it would change matters in any way.

But it did. Incredibly. Both Becky and I needed many "mental-health days" during the following months, but because of what she said to me that night, I could be myself again, be whole, be real. That night I had already plummeted far over the waterfall's lip, but it was Becky's arm that reached out and caught me. She stopped me. And now because of her loyalty and love we climbed out, up the terrible rocks. We never slipped because there were two of us. And now, forever, there are two of us. ▣

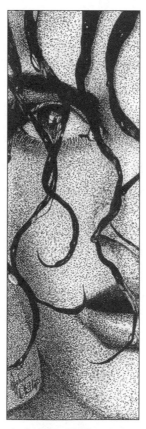

Art by Johna Phillips

Not My Parents

by Natalie R. Studwell

Not my parents
my parents had
straight teeth
My parents did not smoke
but one evening they sat me down on the couch.
I was in the middle with
Dad on one side
Mom on the other and
my mom said we were going to get
a Divorce.
Courtney's parents were divorced
her dad had
long dirty hair and yellow teeth
Her mom smoked and wore tight jeans.
When Courtney's dad came over
they snapped bitter words at each other
Not my parents
They said it's okay you can
tell us what you think. I
Stared at the coffee table
my voice shook as I explained
my theory
You guys aren't like Courtney's parents.

But then I remembered
As I lay in bed some nights
my father's voice
exploding
through the apartment.
I had known something was wrong.
When we got up from the couch
My face was wet.
I realized
It could be my parents

Sympathy and Silence

Fiction by Valerie Ross

Sometimes my brother Kyle would sit at the window seat, watching the girls who lived across the street. They would jump rope and sing a chant, and he would open his mouth like he was going to say something, but he always closed it again.

When he was four, Kyle still hadn't spoken. He had made the gurgling noises all infants make. He had said goo and ga in the trademark way of toddlers, but then it stopped. His only noises were yawns, sighs, chuckles, wordless wails like a banshee incapable of speech and a disgusting sound when he chewed with his mouth open. For a while, Mom thought he could talk and did so in the privacy of his room, but she discarded that idea after monitoring his room with a baby intercom and hearing only raspy breathing.

The summer he was four, I had just finished eighth grade. My two best friends were away at camp. June lasted for years. It was usually too hot to go anywhere and too boring to stay home. So that left me with Kyle.

Don't get me wrong; Kyle was a sweetie. He had the kind of big brown eyes that make puppies irresistible. When he saw a stranger crying, his face stretched with sadness. He'd tiptoe into our backyard, snatch violets that grew wild and present them to Mom with a flourish that made her smile. But he was four years old. The difference between four and fourteen is big enough that we didn't have much in common. There was one thing I was incredibly interested in: Kyle learning to talk.

I heard neighbors say we weren't the best family to learn from. They were right. My father's mother, who lived with us after her husband died, thought formal speech a distraction from her extremely important thoughts about things like dinner and naps. She only communicated in grunts, squeaks and gestures. Or at least Dad said that was her reason. Some of the doctors said that was Kyle's reason, too—he didn't want to learn, but I didn't believe them.

Dad himself had invented an interesting dialect. He spoke in half sentences, unless the sentence was very short. And he called everyone "Sport" or "Chum." A typical sentence was, "It's too nice out to stay inside, sport." Mom spoke oddly, too, agreeing and disagreeing with noises. She would speak sometimes, but usually only hello or good-bye, a name or a short sentence. Unlike Grandma, she didn't think words were a nuisance; she just thought sounds were easier.

When Kyle was very little, my speech was cluttered with "likes" and "ums," but when it became clear Kyle had a problem with language, I began to speak slowly and carefully. I figured if Kyle were going to learn to talk, I would be the one to teach him.

I seemed to be the only one who wanted to help him. Mom and Dad worked hard at first, but as the months passed, so did their enthusiasm. When he didn't respond, they would grip their hands together until their knuckles were white or grind their teeth. They became resigned that something was wrong with Kyle. No doctor could figure it out. His left brain functioned normally; he had outstanding hearing and could understand others. But he remained silent. They talked to him using small words and short phrases, but even these attempts were half-hearted. Mostly they just ignored him.

After Mom or Dad would try to help him, Kyle would retreat to his closet. He kept a flashlight and blanket in there. I'd knock, and usually he'd let me in. We'd snack on chocolate chips and I'd tell him about school, life and how much I wanted to go to Alaska, always trying to get him to respond. It never worked. Sometimes when I knocked I'd hear muffled crying, and on those days I'd walk away, wondering what made him so sad.

One morning that summer, Kyle and I got up early to go to the woods. This year I was allowed to go without an adult. We were so excited that neither of us had a problem getting up early. The adults were early birds and Kyle and I usually ate hours after them, but that morning we joined them. "Well, it's nice to see the two of you awake so early this morning, Sport," Dad smiled sarcastically. He rarely spoke directly to Kyle.

I ignored Dad's tone. "It gets hot; we wanted to be in the forest when the heat hits. Right, Kyle?"

Kyle nodded.

"It's supposed to be quite hot today. The two of you might want to wait and go tomorrow," Dad sipped at his coffee. Kyle's face fell, so I quickly said, "Oh, no, we don't mind, really."

"Mm," said Mom in disapproval.

Grandma grunted from her chair and I passed her the milk, splashing some on the table. She hissed. I kept glancing at Kyle, silently begging him to speak.

"Lemonade?" Mom asked. Since we would be gone all day, she insisted on packing us lunch.

"Yeah, sure. That'd be great. Okay, Kyle?" He nodded.

Mom opened the fridge and cold air blasted onto Grandma, who scooted her chair away.

I held our lunch, and Kyle had the lemonade. He swung it back and forth during our two-hour walk. His small legs and curiosity forced us to take a leisurely pace.

Kyle loved the woods. We didn't go very often, but when it was suggested his mouth would peel into a smile and he would nod vigorously. Once they were in sight, he moved as quickly as he could. He had to sniff every flower, breathing in the smell of sunlight hitting petals. He would touch the rough bark of each tree, grinning the entire time, and grab my hand to run around the edge of every clearing. That was just like him, to love the little things. He was the one who cried over the baby bird that couldn't fly. Normally, going to the woods was not interesting, but with Kyle ecstatic at my side, I enjoyed it, too.

This particular trip, Kyle reviewed six clearings before he found the one he liked for our picnic and made sure it was soft and free from snakes. We spread the blanket, smoothing out the wrinkles. Neither of us was hungry, so I sat, the sun in my eyes. I turned over to lie on my stomach, disturbing the blanket. Kyle busied himself smoothing it. I smiled at his childish, industrious manner, his world overtaken with hunting for wrinkles.

It was so peaceful, lying in the sun, my little brother beside me.

"Isn't it gorgeous, Kyle?" I started to pick at the grass, but he slapped my hand. I forgot how closely he guarded his precious forest. "It seems much prettier than last year. Maybe the sun is bigger."

Kyle shook his head and laughed, dimpled cheeks curling up to let the sound out. As he laughed, I felt a sadness. Most kids his age would have said I was silly or screamed, "No!" But Kyle just laughed. Sometimes talking to him was like talking to my teddy bear late at night; I could tell all my secrets and receive only sympathy and silence. "Kyle, I wish you would talk. I know you can. Mommy and Daddy and the doctors all say no, but it's in you." I sat up abruptly and turned toward him. He became upset with the wrinkles I had created, but I grabbed his hands so he would pay attention.

I spoke in a gentle voice. "What's wrong, Kyle? What are you hiding? It's not as though you don't know what to say. You must have a million things to say by now. Why don't you say anything, Kyle?"

He looked like he was going to cry. Just as he almost did, he glanced sadly at me. "I just wanted to get all the words right first."

I stared at him for a second. Then tears streamed down my face. I grabbed him to me, then pushed him away to look at him again. "Oh, Kyle, why didn't you talk before? I wouldn't have minded if you didn't know the words."

Kyle wiped tears from my face with his sleeve. "I wanted you to think I was big."

"You were plenty big, Sweetie. But you're bigger now, lots bigger, okay?" He nodded.

I was suddenly puzzled. "Why didn't you speak for Mommy and Daddy?"

"I talked to you because you wanted it more."

"Why did you think that?" It was true and we both knew it. He watched me solemnly before he sat carefully on my lap.

"You cried at night and they didn't."

It was like him to know that. I pressed my cheek to his sweaty blond hair. "Oh, Kyle," I mumbled.

Kyle and I didn't warn Mom and Dad that he'd talked. When we got home, he just said, "Hi, Mommy. Hi, Daddy," as though he'd spoken a hundred times before. They started screaming and jumping like they were in pain, but then I noticed the grins spread across their faces, and they squashed him in an embrace.

They couldn't stop talking to him. When he tried to watch his favorite cartoon, they talked so much he couldn't stand it. When the two of us closed ourselves in his closet, they nearly went crazy, asking him questions through the door.

Kyle and I knew I had heard his first words. We never told them. 🔲

My Father's Binding Strings

by Val Koutmina

Early that Saturday morning
the air was cool.
It brushed a sky the color of peaches.
The neck of my black woolen sweater constricted,
binding me.
My father's pallid face,
still creased with pillow marks,
stared from across the worn wood of the kitchen table.
One of his legs twitched nervously;
its swish penetrated the silence.

I suddenly realized how much he knew,
how little he understood.
What had gone on last night
was beyond his steely gaze.
He frowned.
I smiled in my mind.

His stare grew heavy under my prim smirk.
My blue eyes glistened with the slivers of
    morning sunlight

Splashed across the table.
He didn't understand
How my heart had soared in the balmy August night.
How it ran with me
Out of the house in the early hours of morning.

He rambled on
And on about his childhood—
It was nothing like my wild one.
There is nothing at all in common between us:
no strings to tie me down to his restrictions.
This realization strikes me
as I drift further away from his lecture
and deeper into my daydream.

Summer Lull

by Sierra Pope

If I could preserve this night as my memory of childhood, I would be able to look back satisfied. It is a sultry July evening. Outside, my golden retriever is enjoying the breeze stirring the humid air. The wall clock in the dining room is ticking even measurements of the hours I spend with my family in the living room. Though I cannot see it, I know there must be a moon and that later it will leave shafts of light on my floor, enhancing the shape of my skylights and moving across my sleeping face as the Earth turns.

I am sitting in the living room, surrounded by soft yellow light and ceiling-high shelves of books. This is a room that bombards the senses. There are novels of every color covering two of the walls, and under the slow whirring fan is a billiards table; three striped and two solid balls are remnants of an unfinished match. The musty smell of the books merges with the aroma of a kitchen full of broccoli quiche and chocolate shortbread. This is familiarity for me. It is comfort.

Chamber music plays on the record player, a sad, slow melody perfect for a warm summer's night. I close my eyes and hear the violin and sitar play together, separating, harmonizing, the sound waves blending like rings of raindrops on a lake. I am reading a book about the amazing ballet pair Nureyev and Fonteyn, and am absorbed in the world of grace and elegance, of black-and-white pictures. My hair, long enough to reach my waist, is still wet from a shower. I have curled my legs up into my chair like a small child, perching sideways, my head resting on my knees.

My mother sits in a chair near the south-facing window with brown reading glasses on the tip of her nose. There is a glass of iced tea on the coffee table, forgotten now in the third chapter of a southwestern mystery paperback. I watch and wonder if she is aware of the world around her, of the cat weaving about her feet, or if the book has consumed all her attention. This is often how it is with books. On the window a swarm of insects tries to reach the light above her shoulder. There is a hum, a tapping, as they fly in figure eights on a ceaseless quest for the lamp.

My father is near the record player, looking at the back of *The White Album* and checking off titles on a continuous list of music in our collection. We have hundreds of albums, from Mike Oldfield to Chicago, Donovan to Beethoven, and I have heard them all. My father has spent his life collecting our literary and musical library. We have a record of this century without numbers; ours has the poetry, accounts and songs of different eras.

No one is speaking tonight. The world has a hush about it, as if there were an unwritten rule not to break the summertime spell. The notes of Sonata No. 3 in A Minor, the rustle of pages turning, the trill of the crickets and tremors of the spruce trees—these sounds combine to make a cacophony that rises, fills the room and finally neutralizes into a lull.

I look up from my finished book, and slowly the room forms before my eyes. For a minute I sit and watch all this, taking in the music and colors. The tone in this room is like a crackling fire, something in the background that I know is there but my mind has tuned out. If this evening had been six months ago or the summer before, I could have stayed for hours in that peaceful room.

Something has stirred within me, though, and I am not content to sit still here. This atmosphere, like the rest of my peaceful childhood days, has to end. Somebody will shut the damper and interrupt everything.

As quickly as possible, as if to lessen the tension of breaking our quiet summer lull, I stand and begin to walk out of the room. I speak, and the sound waves splash against the air.

"I'm going to bed."

My parents look up, and, as I leave the room, I hear my mother say, "Don't stay up too late, please."

I leave this request unanswered and tread up the stairs. I am still quiet.

That summer evening was the last time I experienced such a connection with my family and this world around me. I don't sit with them in the living room anymore. Times have changed, and I have taken on the role of traditional teenager—listening to loud music, talking on the phone and on the computer. I am isolated from the rest of the household. It is a missing piece of me. It is the negative side of growing up.

My Hans Christian Andersen and Madeline L'Engle books have changed to Ayn Rand and George Orwell; my long hair has been cut to conventional length. My wristwatch and calendar say I have aged less than a year, but my own sense of time passing has experienced eons. I have lived and changed by several years since I sat in peace in the living room, since that kind of night was enough.

I can barely hear the music downstairs, but I know everyone is there, together. Perhaps in a few years my clock will slow back to normal and everything won't happen in such a blur. I will be able to appreciate the time of books and music, family and familiarities, calm and comfort. As it is, these teenage years seem to be the very lonely "best years" of my life. ▣

Photo by Paulina Alenkina

Landscapes:

Stories of Grandparents

Art by Betsy Clauss

My Pépère

by Angie M. Drouin

As I peer around the plants, I scan the field with eyes squinting from the brilliant sun. Seeing no one, I pop three deliciously sweet strawberries into my mouth, savoring each one. Then I stand and begin to search for the next inviting plant, but find that I have devoured every one of the "perfect" strawberries. Deciding to change spots, I see him—a tall, husky man kneeling on one knee, his balding head covered with a hat and his eyes hidden behind sunglasses. I watch him. Drops of sweat bead on his face. The sun is beginning to be too much for him. He is amazing as he picks each strawberry with a precision only he possesses. Within a fraction of a second, he is able to select the most scrumptious berries.

I trot over and proudly show him my bucket, which is half full. He smiles with approval. I feel good until I glance at his bucket, which is overflowing.

I pop a few more strawberries in my mouth and he says, "Well, that should do it." Once we have our berries weighed, he hands the clerk the money with large, wrinkled hands. I race him to the car. He does not run, and it doesn't matter. We begin the long journey home. There is no music and not much is said, yet the silence is welcomed. I glance at the man sitting next to me and wonder how old he is. In my childish mind, I imagine ninety, at least. He senses me staring, turns to me and smiles. Ahh, that smile. It is one in a million. Through his smile, you can see it all. The warmth and love this great man possesses is startling.

Strawberry picking used to be an annual event. It was always sad to see the berry season end. Today the sun doesn't seem to shine as brightly, and it looks as if we won't go strawberry picking together this year. I am much older now, and so is he. Right now, I am not with that great man; instead I am with my sister on the way to see him. We walk through the revolving doors, down the hall and to the elevators. His room number is E205. I see him lying in an all-white bed with tubes everywhere. He no longer looks like the man I picked strawberries with.

Art by Elena Fox

Now, he looks like a defenseless, old man whose health is beginning to fail.

"Hi, Pépère," I say. In almost a whisper he replies, "Hello, Angie." I don't ask how he's doing because, honestly, I don't want to know. I look at him and say nothing. My mother and grandmother are there, too. He is doing his best to make conversation, but no one is sure what to say. For me, I feel as if I am in a dream. It seems utterly impossible for such an awesome man to become so helpless. It's terrifying.

After a short time, we must leave. I kiss him good-bye and tell him I love him. Reluctantly, I leave. My sister and I get in the car for the journey home. There is no music and not much is said, yet the silence is deafening and painful. I throw in a tape and crank up the radio, hoping to drown out the pain I am feeling.

Good night, Pépère. ▣

Treasures

by Elizabeth A. Moseman

She stands at the door, waiting, watching.
The wind plays with her wispy white hair,
twirling it in front of her wrinkled face.
Her eyes are the color of winter skies:
light, washed-out blue.
We walk down the path to her house,
lugging our various suitcases.
She welcomes us,
and we present our faces for a kiss
against her whiskered face.

She says, "My, how you children have grown."

She totters around her house,
mumbling to herself,
and we ask her questions about all her antiques.
She tries to answer,
but forgets the words,
and fumbles,
trying desperately to think.
We try to help,
but we don't know the words
to help erase that wild scared look on her face.

She says, "My, how you children have grown."

The next morning,
before we leave,
she gives us presents,
glittering beads and necklaces
from her travels
in the days when she was young.
We point out different ones we like or admire,
and sometimes it's one of her special ones.
And that wild look comes into her eyes,
and her hand closes tightly on her treasure.

She says, "My, how you children have grown."

Then she opens an old dresser,
to expose drawers of fabric,
all knitted,
some neatly stitched together.
In four colors,
they sit unfinished.
The four of us look at each other,
and she sees the glance that passes between us.
Her eyes grow soft and she reaches in to hand
*   them to us.*

She says, "My, how you children have grown."

She cradles them in her arms,
the pieces a patchwork of color.
She seems reluctant to give them up.
She tells how it took her over twenty years to knit them all,

in the far-off places when she traveled.
And I realize,
her past is woven into those bright colors,
the yarn,
twisted into a network of
tangled memories.

She says, "My, how you children have grown."

We hold out the bags,
and she drops the pieces in,
and the piles of even squares
become disorganized.
Her eyes start to take on that wild look,
and she says again how long they took,
and her memories of the places she'd been.
As the squares fall into the bag,
she feels that her memories are slipping away,
and clutches at the bag.

She says, "My, how you children have grown."

When we leave,
we carry with us
her unfinished afghans,
her jumbled memories,
and I finally know what to do.
I will sew up your afghans, Grandmother,
and stitch your memories back in order.
And I will say,

"My, how I have grown"

We Planted the Garden Alone

by Erienne McCoole

The rising sun peeked into my window and gently woke me. Robins and chickadees competed for airtime with wings that sounded like my mother's wash flapping in the wind. Their songs were long and shrill; dozing was out of the question. The insistent click of my dog's toenails on the hardwood floors and her cold, wet nose pushed into my face was the final encouragement I needed to get out of bed.

As I pulled on my oldest jeans and most-loved sweatshirt, I heard my mother's knees crack, telling me I was not the only one awake. We went downstairs together to eat muffins and fresh fruit with my brother. The morning paper rustled as he searched for the comics. We ate quickly because this was "garden day."

Tilling the soil was my mother's job. The machine she used was heavy and loud. When she cut the engine, our ears rang for several minutes, reminding us that even with plugs, tilling the soil the old-fashioned way would be better. My brother and I put up a fence to keep animals out. Everyone had a hammer to pound the fence into the soft, dark earth. Then it was seed time. The rows had been carefully planned and everyone had a vegetable to plant. This was our quietest moment. We all looked at our magic hammers and knew this garden was different.

The "magic hammer" was my grandfather's idea. Everything grew large if planted with a magic hammer from my grandfather's toolbox, and he had a seemingly endless supply. No grandchild was without one. He would fill our garden time with laughter and our ears with stories of him on the "old wooden ships." He explained how hard it was to "grow good vegetables" on their decks. When we were little, we believed him. Now, we adore him.

He did not come to help us today. He is old, he says, and does not like to leave his house for too long. The man who once went to sea on submarines for nine months at a time is afraid to leave his front porch.

His voice is softer now and his stories, if he can remember them, are slower, filled with the sounds of the sea more than the sights he saw. His gray-blue eyes go out of focus as he relives the times when he was younger and his hands did not hurt. His silences are longer and more frequent as his mind goes to sea without his body.

This silence, his silence, fills my ears as nothing else ever will. I can see him getting old, that is true, but the worst is hearing him get old. This is almost more than I can bear.

So today we planted our garden. We put up our sun-faded red fence and accented its corners with my mother's collection of exotic birdhouses. And when we made holes with our magic hammers, we thought of my grandfather and how he was not coming. When we pushed in the seeds, we remembered his laughter. When we covered the seeds with dirt, we knew our garden days with him were in the past. The silence around our conversation was because one of us was missing.

After the work was finished, I sat back and looked at the blue sky and watched it darken to twilight. I could almost hear the ocean getting rougher, as if one of Grandpa's storms was building. As the screen door closed softly behind me, I wondered if Grandpa was still sitting on his porch. I wondered if the light in his eyes had faded a little more today. With the thought of that light fading forever and the sounds of his sea in my mind, I asked Mom if we could plant a garden at Grandpa's house tomorrow. She must have heard the same storm at sea because she smiled and said, "Of course." ▣

Photo by Noelle Colby DiLorenzo

Ready to Listen

by Patricia Pelczar

There is a little white house on the corner of a tidy little street. In that house sits a slightly chubby man in a plush green rocking chair. I can hear him speaking in his low, even voice as if he were here with me now.

The voice is highly intelligent even though the speaker does not have a college degree. The hands that move so gracefully with the voice are patient and caring, yet these hands have never held placards in a demonstration. The sophistication reflected in the eyes is evident although those eyes have never been to the opera or ballet.

That voice has helped me out in calculus without ever having studied it. Those hands, which rocked me as a baby, helped stop a Christmas tree from falling on me as a teenager. Those eyes have seen Europe in a battlefield. They have watched one president's assassination and another's fall from grace. The falling of a wall, a legendary trial and other historical events have also passed before them.

The voice, hands and eyes have taught. I have learned of life before my time. The little boy who used to let black widow spiders crawl up his hand is now my teacher. The young adolescent who had to pay, in his final grade, the price of declining to play on a teacher's baseball team is now my teacher. He has taught well.

There is more to a worthwhile life than college degrees and Nobel prizes. Life is not all high society, money and power. Life is people. Life is sharing: passing down traditions and memories. Life is having the wisdom to be happy with who you are. Neither all the degrees nor all the money in the world can give a person this wisdom or this happiness; we have to find them on our own.

My grandfather still sits in his plush green chair in his little white house. He is ready for his next lesson, and I am ready to listen and to learn. 回

True Beauty

by Cheryl Brewer

True beauty is not high cheekbones, long legs or bulging biceps. You can only find it if you look with an open mind and heart. You don't see it often, and then usually only for a split second, but it's always there, just out of sight—like the one time I saw true beauty.

My grandfather was in the hospital for a relatively simple operation, but there were complications. Pappy had a weak heart (his first heart attack occurred before I was even born), but he was tough and outlived most of his brothers. He also had kidney problems; one doctor wanted to put him on dialysis, while the heart specialist argued that Pappy's heart couldn't handle that stress. Over the next three weeks, Pappy was moved in and out of intensive care many times.

Through it all, my grandmother was there with him every day, going home only for clean clothes and showers, and sleeping at a nearby hospitality house. She was exhausted but didn't want to leave him, even though he had people with him at all times. MawMaw felt Pappy needed her near while he was ill, and I think she needed to be near him, too. After fifty-six years of marriage, you get attached.

The doctors did nothing to relieve her worry. They kept relaying different stories—the lung specialist told us Pappy would die because he wouldn't be able to breathe; a few minutes later, the heart specialist told us he had held Pappy's hand, and that Pappy was as strong as a horse and would be fine. I wanted him to be all right, so I believed that doctor.

Imagine our family: children, grandchildren, siblings and friends who hadn't slept for many days. We were all stressed out and no one looked great. Then I glanced across the waiting room and saw my grandmother. I don't know what it was, but she looked so beautiful. Telling my mother to look at her, I asked, "Isn't she pretty?" My mother looked at me like I was crazy. "Sure, baby," she agreed.

MawMaw seemed to be glowing, with a warmth around her. I know it sounds corny, but she looked strong, determined and incredibly loving. Ten minutes ago she was just MawMaw, with gray hair, wrinkles and rumpled clothes. Now she was vibrant. Her hair was a beautiful silver and her wrinkles were laugh lines. Maybe the hospital's smell of death had gone to my head, but I realized it wasn't her physical aspects that suddenly made her so beautiful, it was the love coming from her—love for her children, grandchildren, friends and, most of all, her love for Pappy. Her beauty was in her emotions, her attitude toward people and life, and I saw all this in an instant. I understood the image I saw was inside her, and I was getting a peek. I kept staring at her, afraid I would lose my new perception if I looked away. I was afraid something would blind me to that beauty, take away my insight.

The next day when my grandmother went home to shower, Pappy died. They were so close, she knew before she got back to his room. She just kept walking toward the doctor and my parents, but by the time she got to them she was crying, almost uncontrollably. I watched her as all that beauty turned to hurt and anger and despair. I lost my vision. That's why physical beauty now seems so trivial to me. I've seen true beauty—it's love. ◙

Photo by Nick Calcaterra

Trip with Papa

by Laurel L. Oberg

Many people have influenced me during my seventeen years, but no one has had a greater effect than my grandfather, William Joseph Scanlon, or Papa, as I called him. Since my grandparents cared for me while my mother taught school and my dad did his computer work, I've spent a lot of time with my papa.

My earliest memories center around my grandfather's sense of humor and how he always brightened everyone's day. One of our favorite outings was to the grocery store. My grandmother would get me all dressed up, perky bow and all. As the little queen, I'd ride in the carriage, surveying my subjects. Papa would always stop to talk to the managers and tell them jokes. Soon they knew his name and mine, as did many of the cashiers. People were always glad to see us; their eyes would light up as they waited to hear Papa's newest story. My older sister and I were frequently the stars of his tales, and he made everyone feel as though they had observed what he described with all his vivid details.

Other days the bank was our destination. After making his deposits he would inquire about a job for his granddaughter. I would hide under the desk, listening to the adults talk. They would say, "Well, how old is she?" Then he'd fish me out from under the desk and plunk me down on the counter. He'd say, "What do you think? Will she do? She's really good with money, you know." The bank tellers would roar with laughter and give me a lollipop. I'd be so embarrassed and I'd say, "No, Papa. Nana won't let me work, I have to take my nap!" He'd laugh, make his little smirk, and out the door we'd go as the tellers waved and told us to come back soon. This little drama was enacted twice a month, at least, but everyone involved loved it.

Off we went, Papa and I, to do more errands and spread more happiness.

Probably the ladies who enjoyed our visits the most were the secretaries at my pediatrician. My doctor was great with kids but stern and demanding toward his staff. If the doctor kept us waiting, Papa would say, "Larry, we're on the clock here. Let's get a move on." The secretaries loved when Papa bossed him around. When my mom would call, they'd say, "We'd prefer Papa brought the girls for their appointments." They loved to hear his banter.

Papa has shown me one of the most important aspects of his world—making others happy by brightening their days with laughter. 回

Wrapping

by Amanda Coffin

Mom was on the phone
tears on her red face
not speaking, she just stood

My ears covered with four-year-old hands
somehow her sobs still entered
bounced into my head from crazy angles

I pressed the scrap of wrapping paper against my head
keep those bad sounds out,
pretty pattern make my world sweet again

I took the wrapping paper from my ears
wrinkled in my sweaty little palms
and for just one moment it was perfect

But then she finally said the words to me
and sounds suddenly collided
and thoughts crashed into each other

I knew we would never visit him in Maine again
and Poppy was gone
and the wrapping paper hadn't kept it out.

The Transformation

by Jaime Koniak

When I was little I really didn't see her as lonely. From a ten-year-old's point of view, she seemed independent. I would step into her shaggy, avocado carpeted world and be greeted with freshly squeezed orange juice, boiled chicken and outstretched arms. It was the place where I met and fell in love with Grandma, sitting on her green bedspread, listening to tales of when she was my age. It was the place where I learned to like *The Young and the Restless*. It was the place where I was the most special little girl in the world.

She had always lived alone. I thought that made her strong. Grandma, in my eyes, was a role model, her own woman. I marveled at how she had gotten her hairset down to a science, wrapping her head in toilet paper, mummifying herself for the night. When I stayed with her, her hollow apartment echoed with my laughter as I watched her take out her "teeth" and make funny faces in the mirror. She was embarrassed for anyone else to see her, but merely to evoke a smile from her biggest fan, she permitted me to watch.

I would sleep at her apartment while my mom and dad stayed at a hotel down the road, for Grandma's "house" was life for one: one bedroom, one couch, one bath-room, one table. I slept with her in the king-sized bed that usually remained half-tucked in.

We bonded, we smiled, we hugged, we glowed.

A few years ago Grandma became disoriented. A few years ago a little girl grew up. Living alone with no one to lean on, Grandma could no longer stay in her avocado home. She had to be moved to a nursing home. She still has her life for one, but she now lives with many other "independent" souls.

Her hands gripping the cold, steel banisters, she is helped down to the cafeteria for freshly squeezed orange juice in the morning and maybe an occasional boiled chicken dinner. She sits in her room talking to photo-graphs and watching TV. She no longer watches *The Young and the Restless*. She doesn't know how to change the channels, and there's no one there to do it for her.

I still speak to her every Sunday; I'm interested in all that she does. Though now I'm the strong one, the inde-pendent one. Grandma isn't independent or strong at all. Grandma is lonely. And the carpet isn't avocado; it's gray. ▣

Singing "The River"

by Megan Farnsworth

I sat alone in the back of our family van, surrounded by the sleeping bundles of my brother and sisters. Their round faces protruded from fuzzy blankets, but sleep evaded my weary body as the long drive continued into the dense night. Two orbs of light penetrated the stiff darkness enough to illuminate the narrow, never-ending road ahead. The engine purred beneath me; the van rocked softly on its frame while the vents expelled an encasing breath of warm air. Steam condensed in small billows on the long rectangular windows lining the interior.

Intermittent raindrops splattered across the window, but the thunder was strangely silent. Tumultuous lightning raged to the earth, screaming white rays of light piercing the darkness. In awe I watched while my mind reeled back to July. . . .

The air outside had been sticky as the sun beat down. Flies danced drunkenly around the neatly clipped lawn. Inside the nursing home, gleaming linoleum floors slapped unforgivingly against my Keds. In front of me, Great-Grandma Agnes hunched over her walker. Blue veins rose across her arthritic, age-spotted knuckles, and gnarled hands tightly gripped the plastic handles of her support, her hair swept in snowy wisps about her wrinkled face. Her swollen ankles dragged heavily as she inched her way up the hall. Her sons steadied her on either side. Behind me I saw my uncles, aunts and cousins. The younger generations had come to visit Grandma Agnes. The entire family trailed behind her into the cafeteria. The bitter smell of coffee was strong. We gathered around Great-Grandma as my grandpa's strong arms lowered her gently into a waiting wheelchair.

The splash of bright flowers on her dressing gown held my eyes and I glanced at her face for a sign of acknowledgment. Her deep hazel eyes were clear and comprehending as she looked at each of us. For a moment the silence was uncomfortable and oppressive, but a voice from behind appeased me, "Sing, girls, sing for Grandma." My ten-year-old cousin stood next to me, her tan face bewildered. Its usual radiance was drowned by her fear. I began to sing, my voice insignificant in the open room. Soon all of the great-granddaughters joined me.

"The River," a song made popular by Garth Brooks, flowed through the nursing home. Orderlies gathered and patients cocked their heads. The fear was gone and my heart soared with the increasing intensity of the song. I saw tears glisten in my mother's eyes and felt the reassuring weight of Grandpa's hand against my shoulder.

Too many times we stand aside and let the water slip away. 'Til what we put off till tomorrow has now become today. So don't you sit upon the shoreline and say you're satisfied. Choose to chance the rapids and dare to dance the tides. I will sail my vessel till the river runs dry.

Our voices ceased. The song ended with a smattering of applause. Great-Grandma's eyes were large and dark behind her thick horn-rimmed glasses showing ninety-seven years of hard work, love, heartache and life. Her pale moist lips curled into a smile, and she touched her hands together twice in recognition. Our clan's arduous trek down the hall to her room seemed shorter. There was a slight bounce in my step and a warm calm within me. Once she was situated on the high hospital bed, we all took a turn hugging her fragile body. I glanced back to see her head touch the pillow and her hands clasp peacefully at her waist. . . .

A curve in the road swept away the memory of my last visit with Great-Grandma. My eyes focused once more on nature's display. The small beads of dew gathering on the window's edge contrasted with the steely chill of night and the secure comfort of the van. It had been a long drive. After hours of driving, our destination felt near. Her funeral would be tomorrow. My eyes drooped. I settled into my own comforting blanket and let the roll of the van lull me into a deep, unfettered sleep. 回

Photo by Matt Schafer

Born Ready

by Matt Wiesenfeld

There it was. Clashing, crashing and rumbling toward me every second. I looked up at my grandpa and hoped for the best. I took a deep breath and advanced into the "stormy swimming pool." It was time now for me to show my true colors of beach bumness. An ocean and a ten-year-old boy had come together at last to complete the puzzle. I was officially going to learn how to body surf, a special trait of the Wiesenfelds for years.

The Beach Bum Club included my grandpa, my father and my brother. I was the missing link. My orange- and blue-striped bathing suit glistened from the rays of the hot sun. This was my lucky bathing suit. While wearing it, I had skimmed a rock seven skips, caught a winning football catch and boogie boarded for the first time.

"Okay, we've gone through all the steps on the ground," my grandpa told me. "Now, let's do it, Matty!"

"Are you sure I'm ready?" I asked, my last words before entering what could be my final dip in the ocean.

"You are a Wiesenfeld. You were born ready!" he exclaimed.

My toes touched the incoming tide I had grown accustomed to throughout the years. The spray of the ocean on my body felt wonderful, almost a sign of reassurance. My grandpa dove into a couple of waves, as I did, until we got to the right point of departure. All that was left was to find the right wave and "ride the big one." *Turn around, crouch down and get a good push off,* kept going through my mind like runners of the local marathon. And then there it was. Perfect in shape, perfect in size and perfect for me.

The wink in my grandpa's eye told me that it was now or never. A quick glance at my bathing suit encouraged me to strive to reach my final goal, no matter how grim the outcome looked. A quick turn was followed by a good crouch. The push off was like a true Wiesenfeld. One minute I was with my grandpa deep in the great sea, and the next I tasted sand. This meant only one thing: I was tasting sand . . . from the shoreline! I had conquered the great wave and, more important, my great fear. Standing there in adoration, I felt at one with the beach, thanks to my grandpa and thanks to my suit. My bathing suit and I have forever become honorary members of the Beach Bum Club. ▣

Only in Photographs

by Lindsay Moss

I

Small and petite; rippled and soft,
A basic old lady, as grandmothers should.
"Navy blue is a color for all seasons."
  She stirs slowly the chicken broth, a lazy
  stove-top whirlpool.
At breakfast her thumb will press to simple
  white ceramic,
Sesame seeds adhere to her thumb then stick
  to her tongue,
The tongue that packs monologue not important
  enough to operate,
The ones which Dad might only know by eavesdropping
  from the womb.
  So she does the laundry and bastes the turkey.
  Shops at King's and reads sales at Bloomingdale's.
She smiles and moans a giddy laugh.
"Ooooh!" she says, a grin lifting a crescent smile,
Stretching cheeks with thread-thick canals.
  When she speaks her voice is thin,
  stitching through the air to fasten the atmosphere,
Appreciated but not acknowledged.

Dad poses with her in frames encrusting the
   living room wall,
bodies always posed with slanting angles to the left,
   She says it's her good side,
   My children will never see the right.

II
She exists only in photographs,
Thick, glossy, crimped and fringed around the edge.
Her sepia youth rests within my house in an extinct
   brand of kitsch-patterned album.
Even lawns of grass lie mattress to women and babes
   who play on assumed green.
   Resembles my sister, a little like me.
Now she preens herself for an evening out
She wears in her closeted bathroom a dress I see
   in vintage stores.
Did it smell like attic wool when new?
   Then color claws at my pupil like a putrid, faded
   Wizard of Oz
in depictions of tight-skinned versions of Mom and
   uncles and aunts encircling a dinette.
   Homemade birthday cakes exert mustard-yellow script.
   "Happy Birthday, Mommy."
I cracked her picture years ago;
A thump of bronze on walnut wood, the glass had
   cracked into a transparent puzzle.
   I was sorry, and I think my mother cried.

She Lived Quietly

by Thea Chapin Durling

She was never young to me, but rather a frail, old woman I was expected to love. I respected her; she had a rich history, a full life, having lived for ninety years. She was always there in the background of my life, and here she is as I have known her: Grandmother.

Visiting Grandmother and Aunt Beth was a big event. We had to dress nicely. The long drive was boring until we hit the city. After a struggle through college traffic, we found the small, grassy triangle in front of their apartment.

The elegant brick apartment was clothed in climbing green ivy; the small blocks of ground with trees that sprang out of the broken pavement gave the courtyard the appearance of an overrun jungle. Four stone steps, flanked by wide handrails, brought me to a heavy outer door opening into a foyer with a mosaic floor, mailboxes and doorbells. One deep breath, a push of the bell, and Aunt Beth came hobbling toward us, smiling, key in hand. My best behavior fell over me like a protective shield as I kissed her.

I followed my brothers down the short hall through two doors ("Close them quickly; can't let the cats out!")

into a world of purple lights, pasted-on smiles, snobby Siamese cats and stuffy rooms.

After I kissed Grandmother, my brothers and I headed for the closet. Funny, dark and gloomy as that closet was, it never scared us. We brought out the toys: a trolley with funny, orange, peg-shaped men, a seesaw and other old playthings. I might have been able to coax a cat out of hiding, but the poor Siamese weren't used to rowdy kids. By now, Mom had finished talking to Grandmother and had gone to help Aunt Beth in the kitchen; it was my turn to see Grandmother.

I would sit down and show her my latest stitchery project. It was she who taught me to knit, who gave me her favorite yarn—multi-colored, changing stuff—and whalebone needles. I would talk about school, the boys, Grammy Chapin and Grandmother's life. Sometimes I would take a book from the shelf or flip through one of her old textbooks. I always had to enunciate carefully and speak loudly. Soon after lunch, we would leave or maybe go somewhere with Aunt Beth. It was always a relief to leave the cluttered apartment filled with the high-strung tensions between Aunt Beth and Grandmother.

Then Anna appeared in the apartment. She lived in the same building. A white-haired, slow-moving old woman with an accent and a wonderful oblivion to the tension in the small apartment. It was Anna who took Grandmother out for her walks, and Anna who would convince Grandmother to eat when she wasn't hungry. It was Anna who made Grandmother's last years happier, for these *were* her last years.

Mom relayed the news to us: Grandmother had fallen

outside the apartment and struck her head. She was in a coma and not doing well. We didn't go see her. I didn't want memories of her wrapped into a maze of wires; that wasn't what Grandmother was to me. So the days ticked past. When the news came, we were expecting it. Grandmother had died in a coma, ninety years and seventy-nine days old.

The funeral was a week later. We dressed in our best and drove to the fancy and oppressive church. I endured the obligatory kisses, then quickly followed Grammy down the aisle to a pew. Even though the church was half-empty, we all ended up sitting with Grammy and Grampy. The program read, ". . . in celebration of her life," but the service was long, boring and not at all celebratory. I thought of Grandmother's ninetieth birthday party that past spring. Now *that* had celebrated Grandmother's life: Uncle Bill telling stories with Grandmother cutting in, Grandmother leaning over the cake and becoming young as she blew out the candles and disappeared into the smoke. I realized that was the last time I ever saw Grandmother.

My reverie ended when I rose to leave. My brothers cleaned out the refreshment tables; we said good-bye and left. I rode home, changed into jeans, washed my dress and washed away Grandmother. She is gone; all that remains is my sewing machine, my fast-fading memories, a half-empty apartment and this memoir. Grandmother was always there; she lived quietly, and she left my life quietly and completely. ▣

This Time, Grandpa
by Cassie Olsen

I've been here every day now
The car ride seems perpetual
The silence has endured
And the radio only seems to hum

They've forced you into room after room
And now
Here's just another occupied space
With just another abbreviated name
All the rooms are the same
All impersonal
All so plain I can't imagine living here
How can you endure all the pain?

I wish I could understand you
I wish you could speak
To me
As you once did

There is a murmur of no recovery
And a whisper
That you will not be the same

It is something that I already see
Something you cannot hide

Silence drifts in and out of corridors
Cleaning fluid engulfs the halls
My head is pounding
From the stench or stress
I don't know

What I do know is that I love you
Something I never knew before

We float back
To the waiting room
The room was made
To be comfortable
Somehow
It has missed this goal
The same way I feel

Nothing has been accomplished
And nothing has been silenced
This day-to-day
Repetition
It has gotten us nowhere

Maybe nowhere is better
I thank God
You have not gone anywhere

Realization

by Josh Winslow

On my eighth Fourth of July, I awoke hearing someone calling my father, "Kenny, Kenny, come quickly! Something is wrong with your father!" I ran to the window to see my father sprinting across the lawn and down the path to the cottage next door where my grandfather was staying. The next two hours were some of the longest of my life. I didn't know what was wrong next door, and at that time all I wanted to do was go to the parade. Although my mother, brother and I were quiet, we never heard the ambulance come or go. They did not use their sirens. By then, there was no urgency.

When my father returned, he slowly and quietly told us what had happened. My grandfather had died. My father said, "His death was quick and painless." It took me a long time to realize that my grandfather had been in pain long before his death. . . .

I loved my grandfather so much; I was closer than most kids are to their grandparents. I was born on his birthday. That was special. Once we even celebrated together.

As I grew older, I realized things about my grandfather that I never knew. Although he tried, no one was close to him except the bottle. He was an alcoholic. No one talked about it, and they still don't like to.

I remember finding old bottles deep in the woods around the house. Some I would carefully have to dig out of the dirt that entombed them. Others would be resting on fallen pine needles. I thought they were all great finds, valuable antiques hundreds of years old. Proudly I would bring my newly found treasures to my mother, asking her to wash and display them with her antique bottle collection. I could never understand why these bottles would end up in the trash rather than in the living-room windows. Mine weren't hundreds of years old. Actually they were signs of my grandfather's pain. After draining the bittersweet bottles, he would throw them into the woods as far from his house as he could. He didn't want anyone to know how much he drank because he was so ashamed.

Even when I was very small, there were things that troubled me about my grandfather. I never knew what kind of mood he would be in. The good moods sometimes lasted for weeks, other times less than a day. I thought it was just part of being old.

I remember some wonderful times during hot summer days. My grandfather enjoyed mowing the lawn with his Sears Craftsman mower. Often you would see his bloated body bounce around on the tractor, the same body that as a teenager he could fit through an unstrung tennis racket. His face was shaded by an old pith helmet bought in Bermuda many years before—the kind you see in old photos of big-game hunters shooting elephants. It kept his swollen red nose from getting sunburned. He would put me on his lap and let me steer while the mower did

Photo by Robert Craig

its work. We shared M&M's from his pocket while he sipped on a diet Fresca. Whenever I smell a freshly mown lawn, I remember the tractor rides.

He also liked to work on his antique cars. I loved to go and visit him in the garage while he tried to restore the battered old cars. Sometimes he would let me sit in them and show me how they worked. Once we went for a ride around the neighborhood in his old Model T. He enjoyed putting new life into the seemingly dead cars. Other times when I would go to see him, he would tell me to go away—he was busy. I would hang around trying to be extra good and helpful. I remember thinking I could make him happy by cleaning his garage. I was confused to find the same old, empty bottles in the garage that I always thought were antiques in the woods.

The best time was the birthday we spent together. He gave me the greatest present: a set of real golf clubs, but in my size. They came in a shiny red leather bag. He loved golf, so the clubs were a part of him, and we were both looking forward to the day when we could play together. We were supposed to spend other birthdays together, but he always missed them. Everyone knew why he did not make it.

Today I try to remember the kind and gentle person that was my grandfather and try to forget the part of him that was stolen by the bottle. Sometimes while walking through the woods, my eye will be caught by a gleam of glass, a hidden bottle covered by leaves and pine needles. Before picking it up I try to decide: Is this bottle hundreds of years old, valuable and worth keeping in a collection? Or, is this an empty bottle thrown away, discarded as were parts of his life? ▣

The Final Blow

by Amanda Sengstacken

How frustrating,
How sad,
How unfair,
How maddening.
How terrible
Of that doctor
To tell us such a thing,
How dare he smile
While dealing that final blow?
I'm seeing my own life
Flash before me,
I'm seeing my own pain
Linked with yours
And all I can think about
Is how it is your fault
That you have caused this pain,
That you have done something wrong,
And so I am not talking to you,
Grandma,
Because I am angry at you,
Because you didn't think about my life,
When you caused your own
To end with cancer.

Casualties

Fiction by Emily H. Wilson

Sun is flying off the windows, piercing my eyes. It is harsh and hits me harder than usual. This house is so all-American it makes me sick. I can't stop choking on spit and tears. Three more steps and I'm at the end of the walkway. I hold onto the fence as the wind blows because anything, anything at all, will knock me down. Looking up at the house, curtains blow and wind chimes ring. The whole house is covered with love, and when I take one more step I will ruin it.

I start walking, stumbling, dragging myself up the front path. I turn to the swing set and see Katie.

"Grandpa, come push me?" she calls to me.

I raise my hand as high as it will go, halfway to my shoulder, and keep walking.

"Grandpa!" Katie calls. "Look at the wreath I made for Daddy when he gets home!"

I let my eyes follow the porch floor to the door, across the welcome mat and up. I see the wreath she made. There are buttons and macaroni glued to a piece of green cardboard. I bring my hand up, not to touch it gently, but to drag my fingers through it and rip it into a thousand pieces. I am an inch away when the door opens.

"Oh, good. The washer won't stop running, and Kyle needs to get to soccer practice." Her words trail off as she turns to take an apple pie out of the oven. Its smell surrounds me, like a last happy memory.

The woman, my daughter-in-law, turns to hand me a blue soccer shirt warm from the dryer, then looks for a pair of cleats. When we finally make eye contact, there is that moment, and she knows. It is my eyes that say he's died.

Supporting herself against the stove, she breathes too slowly, then grabs the pie. It's burning her hands; she throws it across the kitchen and sends it flying through that gleaming glass. The pieces fall sharply down. Through the hole in the window, the sounds of Katie and Kyle playing around the corner of the house fly in and hit her as hard as the look on my face had.

"Kyle," Katie screeches, "that's my shovel!" Kyle is giggling. We both watch Katie run across the front yard.

The woman turns to me and whispers, "They said there wouldn't be any casualties; they said it was a safe mission. That's what they said."

Katie is running across the front porch, following the smell of the pie. We hear Kyle chasing her. I look to see her tumble in the door, then turn to see that I am alone in the kitchen. Katie runs to me and wraps herself around my leg.

"Did you see the wreath, Grandpa?" she asks. "Won't Daddy love it?" 回

Double Exposures:
Changes in Our Lives

Photo by Erica J. Hodgkinson

Soon It Will Be Over

by Jennifer Morisson

I run up the two flights of stairs to my room to escape the awful din. The noise is on the first floor, so I escape to my third-floor bedroom. When I reach the top of the stairs, I am winded. I pull my straw chair into the window eave and grab my favorite teddy bear. I turn on my radio and close the door at the bottom of the stairs. I am not allowed to do this, but no one will notice. It is still no use. I can still hear them. I try not to, but it feels like my brain is straining to hear their screams. I can make out some of what they are yelling. It has something to do with my sister not being "the perfect daughter."

No, don't listen. You don't want to hear. It will just make you upset and you know what will happen then. I repeat this over and over inside my head but it doesn't work. I try to concentrate on something else. I look out my window. I see kids playing in the park. They are totally blind to what is happening inside my house. I see neighbors raking their leaves and washing their cars. I see one family getting into a car together. Perhaps they are going apple picking or on a picnic. I remember when we used to do those things. As I look at my neighbors, I wish I could call out and ask for help, but I dare not. I pick up my phone and dial . . . I hang up. Why should I bother someone else with my problems? I remember my dogs are downstairs. The shouts make them quiver. I run down the stairs to rescue them. I risk my life. The shouts get louder. They are shouting and crying. I grab one dog.

"What are you doing? Leave the dogs alone! Get back to your room!"

"Jennifer, help!"

I start to yell and cry, too. There is nothing I can do. I pick up one dog and guide the other up the stairs to my room. After we are in my room, we curl up on my bed. I comfort them.

Soon it will be over. I fall asleep and wake up an hour later. My dogs are still on my bed. The last thing I can clearly remember is hearing a door slamming. I have a terrible headache. It is quiet; I can hear the fall wind blowing through our old house. *This is the way it should be,* I think. I put on a tape of the ocean. It is soothing. I always listen to it after an outburst. I sit back down in my straw chair, which is still in the window eave. I lean back and close my eyes.

A car drives up and I am brought back to reality. I brace myself for the worst. I watch two people get out of the car. It is my father and my sister. The shouts begin again. I still cannot block it out, and this time I begin to cry. I cry for my mom. I cry for my dad. And most of all I cry for my sister. Nothing she does is right for them. I wish they would just let her be. When the shouts stop, my crying is heard. My mother comes to my room to comfort me. I always tell myself I will not talk to her because of how she treats my sister, but I cannot do it. When she leaves, I sit in my straw chair and begin to cry again. My sister comes up.

"It's all right, Jennifer. Everything will be okay. You'll see, some day we will all get along."

I look up at my sister. I see through my tears that she is crying, too. We sit on the floor in the window eave, embracing and crying. ▣

Photo by Megan Galipeau

"Sweet Baby James"

by Michelle L. Cuevas

ometimes you experience a moment, a definitive second, that is beautiful and just perfect. During these moments, I often ponder how wonderful life would be if it were like a movie. You could fast forward through the bad parts, put the confusing times in slow motion and pause on the perfect frames. The human memory serves this purpose in a way, and if I were to pick a recent moment to press that pause button, I would have no trouble choosing.

Emily and Michelle, Michelle and Emily; some call us the Bobbsey twins, even though we look nothing alike. It was great to spend the Fourth of July having fun together. As we descended the driveway, the gravel got into my flip-flops, scraping the tender bottoms of my feet. When we reached the yard, I had to shut my eyes against the stinging smoke of a bonfire. Once beyond it, I saw a small, weathered maroon cabin, a stretch of green grass and a beautiful lake. We stood close to the fire, staring into the orange flames leaping through the coal and wood. The warmth beat against my cheeks and seemed to radiate from the inside out.

We took off our shoes and walked down the small hill. The grass was moist with dew and felt lifeless under my feet. When we reached the water's edge, the canoe beckoned us to sit on its two small seats with peeling paint and go for a ride.

We pushed it into the water, the gritty rocks and dirt scraping its underbelly. Once in the water we hoisted our wooden oars and placed them in the black mirror of water. It did not shatter, but swallowed the oars, making them invisible in the twilight. Then my muscles tightened, and the oar rose with a lapping sound.

We made our way effortlessly to the center of the lake. I couldn't tell when I touched the water; it was the same temperature as the air. The stillness of the water stretched so far that I imagined my fingers creating ripples which spread to the ends of the Earth. The lights, small floating balloons of yellow in the distance, led our eyes to the outdoor concert nearby. The air was filled with the sound of a guitar and the smooth voice of James Taylor crooning "Sweet Baby James." The music blew across the water, floating past my ears in a soft, magical way. We stayed there for a short time, or longer, I can't be sure, because time seemed to be waiting, to be standing still.

Then out of the darkness, a great circle of light exploded in the sky, and golden raindrops fell to the water. The fireworks that night, in that setting, can only be described as how you feel eating a delicious peach. It starts slowly as you sink your teeth into the skin, like when you hear the zipping noise that warns another explosion will soon be in the sky. Then you bite into the fruit with its stringy, soft flesh and juice, and the taste just explodes. Tangy, sour and sweet all at once, like the fireworks illuminating the velvet sky.

The reflections on the water made it seem like we were floating in the air, surrounded by an explosive rainbow. At the moment the fireworks burst, I could see the world in perfect detail: the edge of the water gently lapping the rocks, the brown, weather-beaten dock, my friend's eyes glowing as she smiled toward the sky. That moment was one I will never forget. I know that soon we will be moving in separate directions, yet no matter what I do, or where I go, I find it comforting to close my eyes and let the movie of my life play. I can rewind and pause on that night in the canoe with my friend and enjoy that moment of summer, that moment of life at its absolute finest, over and over again. ▣

Changing Faces

by Cera Drury

full of smiles
sitting on the hardwood floor
her head resting in open palms
dark tendrils of silken hair
cascading, dancing
toward proud shoulders
her oval-shaped face
alive with sincere delight
her voice unrushed
weaving fantasies
of how
one day . . .

we'd be famous
we'd be the special ones
always together
"best friends never part"
she declared
crossing her heart
hoping to die

while I sat
indian-style
my eager head nodding

eyes wide with admiration
silently agreeing to all her hopes
and untamed dreams

no longer a child
she would lie on her bed
staring blankly
listening to
dimmed voices
screeching suicide
clothes ragged
worn yet another day
hair lying limply
on a creased pillow
unsteady hands
grasping a Newport
ashes tumbling on white sheets

while I sat
Indian-style
weaving the fantasies
of how
one day . . .

we'd be famous
we'd be the special ones
always together
"best friends never part"
I reminded her

I can still hear
her laugh
as she crossed her heart

hoping to die

Afterglow

by Danielle Zonghi

 *fterglow . . . I'd like the memory of me to be a happy one. I'd like to leave an afterglow of smiles when life is done.*

I paused as I read the prayer card to my younger sister.

I'd like to leave an echo whispering softly down the ways, of happy times and laughing times and bright and sunny days.

I paused once again, wiped her tears and comforted her with a hug.

I'd like the tears of those who grieve, to dry before the sun, of happy memories that I leave when life is done.

I hugged my sister again and went to my room. I often sat alone thinking about what happened on that Christmas morning. It seemed like yesterday that we were a happy family of five. No sickness. No tears. My life seemed blurry, almost like it had never happened. I tried not to think how my mom had woken me up to tell me that the man I sometimes hated, who had finally accepted our differences, whom I loved more than anything, had quietly passed away that morning. I remember I didn't cry when she told me. I couldn't. I had cried for too many days. I just looked at my mom in shock as though she were telling me a lie right to my face. It couldn't be real; he wasn't *supposed* to die. He was *supposed* to get better.

I felt the tears building.

Why? He was young and had lots of life to live. I tried to forget these thoughts and look back. My mom always told me to remember the happy times that my father and I shared, but these memories were blocked, trapped in the depths of my mind; the thoughts of the past month holding them hostage. All I could think about was that night when we all were sitting with him.

All of us—my mom, my two sisters, and I—sat there crying because my dad couldn't breathe and refused oxygen. I remember holding his hand and feeling him squeeze it while he struggled for each breath we thought could be his last. He'd look me in the eye and then roll his eyes back as if he couldn't take it anymore and just wanted us to let him go. The small dining room turned hospital room with all its medical supplies was hot, and all our faces were red from the tears.

I looked at my mom who had gotten up to grab the oxygen tank and put it on my gasping father. I remember her saying, "Fred, I know you don't want to die. We need you; we love you; spend one last day with us." She started crying as she attached the oxygen to his nose. I had stopped crying and just rubbed my father's hand. My sisters were sniffling and beginning to relax. The room went from a stuffy crying chaotic mess to an almost comfortable place. My sisters and I left as he finally was able to get his one lung working again. It was a constant battle for him; it had been two years since he had his right lung removed, and he had gotten used to it.

I shake my head as a tear falls. These thoughts give me the shivers. A year has passed since my father left his cancer-filled life and moved on to the peacefulness of heaven to look over our family. We still have those times where we look back and cry because we miss him. Today is September seventeenth, the day that he would have turned forty-eight. I try to push the good thoughts through, but I could still hear the horrible cough that filled our quiet house or the mumbles of my father who couldn't remember our names but was glad we were there to comfort him.

It is eerie remembering these events. I shake my head trying to forget, but it doesn't work. I close my eyes and sigh. I sit for a few minutes just thinking. I open my eyes and start reading those words that keep the memory of my father's spirit.

I'd like to leave an echo whispering softly down the ways, of happy times and laughing times and bright and sunny days.

These words make me remember. He would have said something like, "Your life will go on." It comforts me to think he was right. My life has gone on. I'm stronger now, and I have him to thank. I look at his picture on the nightstand, let out a sigh and smile. I walk out of my room full of thoughts of happy times and hard times, but I look at his picture, and I smile knowing his afterglow is with me in my heart, in my mind and in my soul. ▣

Friendly Training

by Lisa Kelly

-5, this is L-7. We seem to have encountered a bit of difficulty in our maneuvering. Shift gears on three—1-2-3, quick, shift! I've got you, change view, bear hard right, one start, now! F-5, shift to gear four, gear four now! Shift, shift, quick, I'm losing you; I'm losing you.

In sixth grade, we invented this game. We had just exited a movie theater on a "double date" with two of our classmates. Instead of "girl talk" about which one was cuter, we sat down at two arcade games, the car type with seats. Neither of us wanted to spend two quarters on a thirty-second game, so we decided to pretend we were astronauts on a mission in outer space. The game occupied us while we waited for her mother.

We kept playing. Every time we were in a bowling alley, arcade or movie theater, we played. She was the only one who knew how to play, and together we mastered outer space. I thought I could always save her by shifting into a different gear, calling mission control or hitting the quarter return button four times. It never occurred to me that I could really lose her.

We've gone to school together for twelve years, meeting in kindergarten. We made our First Communion together, and even made Confirmation side by side. She was the only girl with whom I could play tackle football (until I broke her nose), act out *The Lion King* or give live telecasts from the middle of a severe hurricane, also known as her pool.

Our other friends don't know about my red boots in second grade, how she got sick on "Visit Your Pen Pal Day" in third grade or how her fifth-grade map of Texas didn't have enough rivers. We were in the same Girl Scout troop and quit the same year. I was even her doctor during a tragic fall off the balance beam at our "Olympic Gymnastics Competition" in the woods. When she fell into a tree that ripped a deep cut in her leg, I bandaged it on the spot with duct tape and gauze. She still has the scar and I'm pretty sure now that the cut deserved stitches.

We went on vacations, had sleepovers, took piano lessons and did every project together. (Except at the science fair in third grade when we both made a solar system. Hers was obviously better, but I won because I dressed up like an astronaut. She retaliated in fourth grade with a killer project on weather systems, which surpassed my bird-feeding experiment.) We watched hockey and football games together, made each other Christmas and birthday presents, and even won the title "Best Friends" in our eighth-grade yearbook. We always said we would be friends forever, yet never admitted we were the other's best friend.

She almost moved away in sixth grade. We almost went to different high schools. Those things just didn't happen to us. I thought I could do anything with her by my side. I thought we would go to school together forever. I thought we would always be best friends.

As high school began, we clung to each other, making the same friends and even having lockers near each other. I was lost when I learned we only shared one class together. She didn't play soccer. I didn't play tennis. We made different basketball teams. I asked her to join the church youth group, but she didn't like it. She made other friends and so did I, though we sat together at lunch and still hung out on weekends.

Sophomore year we were lucky even to see each other during the school day. I went on a vacation with other friends. We went to Florida with our softball team, but weren't roommates. I rarely called her and when I did, she wasn't home. My mom asked if we were still friends. I laughed and said of course we were. It never occurred to me we were growing apart.

During junior year, she found a new best friend. I'd call, and they would be at her house. I'd ask her to go out, and she'd say, "Sure, as long as she can come." They were always together in school, with the same classes and activities.

The hardest thing happened in English class. The teacher told us to write about a relationship. I didn't want to write about my best friend and instead wrote about my family. At lunch, classmates began asking about each other's topic. Her new best friend informed us that she was writing about her "new best friend." I was crushed.

I guess I never realized that my new friends probably made her feel neglected, and she probably never thought I felt the same. But there are so many things that only she and I share. Her new best friend does not know about our pretend brothers and sisters, where the best hiding spots in the church choir are, or how to play McDonald's with oddly shaped trees. I thought I had lost her, but in truth, life had won. We aren't little girls who watch Disney movies together anymore, but we can hold onto our memories.

No matter how alike we are, we're two very different people. I'm going to have to learn to let her go sometime, and the training has already begun.

F-5, this is L-7 reporting. If you shift back to second with a quick start, I won't lose you. I've got you; don't worry. I won't forget anything; I won't give you up; I'll never let you go. ▣

Photo by Rebecca Silverman

Watching Rain

Fiction by David Rochelson

Look up," he says, staring proudly at the heavens. I stand, cold and dripping, looking down at my nine-year-old brother. "For real!" he exclaims, smiling broadly without turning to me. "Look up!"

I figure I'll humor him.

"What, you've never watched the rain before?"

I can't help but let a little smile slide through, and I shake my head.

"No, Kevin," I say. "I've never watched the rain."

"Oh," he says, carefully shielding his disappointment. But the grin drips from his face with each successive drop, and we remain in silence for a moment. I scan the horizon for the familiar headlights that will save us from our cold, wet vigil, as he scans the falling drops for bits of chocolate or diamonds. Suddenly, his face lights up again. "Snow?" he inquires.

The smile pokes through again. "No," I say. "Not snow, either."

He pauses again. He's probably never heard of dramatic timing, but he was born with it. "Ever hear how every snowflake is different? You know, no two are alike?"

It's as if some sadistic puppeteer is pulling at the corners of my mouth, back toward my ears and up. "Yeah?"

"That's bull."

I turn to him quickly, stunned but smiling. His head remains locked upward, but his eyes flit toward mine and his smile widens.

"I mean, figure it snows every day, somewhere . . ."

"I know, I know," I say, nodding. "I know what you mean."

"So?"

"So what?" I ask.

He again displays his expertise, pausing perfectly. "So that's bull!"

My laughter erupts, and I can only hope he won't grow up to think words like "bull" are glamorous or can be relied on for cheap laughs. But then, I think, I probably don't have to worry about how this kid will grow up.

He remains focused on the drops that paste his hair down over his eyes, or slide directly into them and overflow onto his cheeks. Despite these inconveniences, he does not abandon his cause and continues to stare at the clouds. I stand there for a moment, watching him, until at last I feel the headlights play across my dripping frame and bite at the corners of my eyes. The station wagon is still a bit down the road, though, and I let him enjoy his solitude a moment more. It feels almost blasphemous to break his concentration, as if he were taking part in some ritual and to speak would disregard his right to religion.

"Kevin?" I say at last. He ignores me, or maybe he is so focused he really doesn't hear. "Kevin? Mom's here."

"Yeah?" he replies, slightly annoyed, cementing my guilt at having encroached upon his Zen. The car turns into the parking lot, and the headlights create an illuminated tunnel through the descending drops. The lamps graze over Kevin, and in this instant he is a photograph, the freckled light frozen across his torso as he gazes intensely (but oh, so innocently) upward. The car rolls to a stop beside us. I hesitate. "Let's go."

He does not respond at first. "Oh," he says simply. He lets one last drop splash between his eyes, blinks, flinches and smiles at me. "Okay," he says, flinging the door open and sliding across the back seat. He does not look back at me, but immediately presses his nose against the glass and stretches his neck heavenward again.

I stand beside the steel cage holding the door, the drops ricocheting off the roof and into my eyes. I look down at the cloth plastered to my shoulders, my arms. I turn my palms over to watch the narrow, swift rivulets form and flow across and over the lines. I tilt my hand so that the water slides down the incline and splashes against the pavement as a concentrated stream. I close my hand and feel the pellets hit each knuckle. I look up and see the drops catch the orange light of the lamppost, slide against one another and crash into my hand, a palm full of diamonds. I smile and look across at my nine-year-old brother, who has shifted his focus from the drops to the Game Boy he retrieved from between the seats. He feels my curious stare and looks over at me inquisitively, as if to say, "Is something wrong?" He raises his eyebrows to repeat his question, but I only smile and shake my head and shut the door. ▣

She Needed Me

by Kathryn Bingle

I always thought that I was a good friend until I met Sarah. At first it was okay because we didn't really know each other. So we talked and laughed. She used drugs, but I didn't really think about that. She never acted like she had a problem, so I didn't bother her about it.

Then our talks got longer and deeper. She talked about her family and all the things she had been through. I, being a good friend, listened and tried to do all I could for her. Meanwhile I talked to her about my problems, and she sympathized with me. We got really close because we had been through a lot of the same things.

She started talking about her drug use, or abuse. Gradually that became the only thing we talked about. Sarah was using almost every day. The longest she would go without drugs was two days. But I stood by her. I told her that she needed help, and we would get into fights over it. I would always back down because I knew that she needed someone and I was the only one there for her. She interpreted my listening to her as meaning I thought drugs were okay. She would try to convince me that I didn't think she had a problem, while I would keep repeating that I knew she did.

I know she used me. Sarah used my friendship to convince herself she was okay. If her straight friend could accept her, then she couldn't possibly have a problem.

Sarah called me one day because she had taken too many drugs and scared herself. If she was telling the truth, she should have died that night. She was shaking, having cold sweats and foaming at the mouth. She wouldn't let me come over or get her help. As her friend I had to help her the best way I knew how. I talked to her for a long time that night. She was incoherent and hallucinating, but I tried to keep her calm. When I hung up, I was mad. I wanted to scream at her and shake her until she understood that she was out of control. I felt she was dragging me down with her. But in order to be a good friend, I thought I shouldn't yell at her because she didn't have anyone on her side. I had to be there— she needed me.

The truth was she didn't need me on her side. She didn't need me just to be there for her. She needed me to give her the truth. She needed me to talk to her parents and get her help. I wasn't being her friend by letting her make me feel responsible for her life or by letting her walk all over me. While I was her friend, I knew that if anything happened to her, I would feel responsible because I didn't try to help her help herself. I was saying it was everyone else's fault and what she was doing was okay.

I haven't really talked to her now for a while, but she knows that I am here when she is ready to admit that she has a problem. Until then she has to take care of herself. I'm not saying that every time it gets tough, drop your friends; it's just that sometimes all you can do isn't going to be enough. Letting go doesn't mean saying good-bye, or "I don't care anymore." It means saying I have done all I can do, and now you must help yourself. ▣

Photo by Sarah Giaccai

We're Free

by Sara A. Foss

I had so much energy
and the sky soared around me
and the moon sliced smiles across his face
and I could run
my arms out like an airplane
and the night was soft and exciting
for it was vacation
and the dead school our playground
and we could sing and think
even simultaneously
in our summer clothes,
our summer life
pariahs no longer
we joined the breeze
swimming over you
kicking dirt in the face of education
our minds drinking dreams,
loosened from teacher's clamps
happy dust we were—
we held our hands and skipped
—we skipped!—
a brilliant idea
engulfing us like the sea

so, impulsive,
(only in the summer)
we scrambled up to the school roof
and, dancing on our prison,
we forced that hatch open
and climbed down
back into the mire.

It was eerie—
only us in the school
and we sprinted around
and screamed;
we did all those forbidden evils,
kicked defenseless lockers,
broke the rules with impunity,
and the night, interested,
followed us down the hall
as we mocked the ugly interior;
the night watched us and laughed with us,
and later, back outside,
freedom in hand
escaped forever,
(at least the summer);
we ran to my house
and caught those fireflies
looked at them
and fed them into the open world
which, unappreciative,
went to work as usual,
neglecting nature's music
and the celebration
of freedom from school.

Our Masterpiece

by Kerri Lynn Morrone

It was huge. No, huge isn't even the word. Enormous? Perhaps. At any rate, it stretched halfway down the beach. Dubbed "Our Masterpiece," it was just that. My brother and I had spent the entire morning and half the afternoon working on our creation, taking only enough time off to dash into the water now and again. But it was worth it.

Turrets of sand towered high above the shoreline, their tiny seaweed flags fluttering in the gentle August breeze. An intricate labyrinth of roadwork weaved its way between the buildings we had constructed with a shovel, pail and an occasional rude word. It was a bonding experience, my brother and I working side by side in the warm sun, exchanging fewer than ten spoken words but sharing our souls at the same time. I don't think I've ever felt as close to my brother as I did that day on the beach.

He was leaving for college the next day. Maybe that's why I felt such an urgent need to have one last hour with him. He was moving on to the real world while I was left behind, still living out my little dream-filled existence.

"Darrell," I said as we sat back on our heels and admired our hard work. "Are things going to be the same when you come back? You've never left the house for more than a few days before. How are things going to be when you come home?"

He was silent for a minute. The chilly ocean spray began to creep slowly up the shoreline, advancing steadily toward the castle we had fabricated to hide ourselves. The sky was tinged a reddish purple, changing the ocean spray from blue to scarlet.

"Darrell?"

The water was lapping at the base of the sandy walls, licking away our foundation, intent on destroying the rest of our little world.

"Nothing ever stays the same," he said softly, and we began to pack our belongings.

Walking down the beach again, toward civilization, we looked back and saw the waves spilling over the tops of the turrets, changing everything, making our own creation seem unrecognizable.

Everything does change, I admitted softly to myself as I watched the water fill our footprints and wash them away. ▣

My Chippy

by Annette K. Pollert

A low, pale light
slips between the slits
Of the blinds, etching
phosphorescent bars
of ice on the cold floor. I
watch those rods of life
attempt to imprison you,
But still you ebb away.

Your chocolate quivering paws,
tender to my touch, are
speckled with silent gray hairs.
Your fur is damp from the
twelve years of friendship
I have recently cried into your
silky coat because
you are ebbing away.

Trusting are your eyes
as we lie, our bellies on the tile,
Noses touching.
I can see the pain of the cancerous
tumors mingle with the

dull arthritic ache of age and
cloud your velvety eyes.
And, you ebb away.

My silent companion, you are
my confidant, my sanity and my heart.
And still you chew with subtle fierceness
On the bones of your life, soon
To be the skeleton of my memory,
Because you are ebbing away.

Photo by Stephen Siperstein

The Carvel Store

by Lollion Chong

The Carvel store in Chinatown was the reason I would go shopping on those Sunday mornings. My father was the shopper in my family, so he, my sister and I would go on these frequent outings. We would get up early and take the subway downtown. The ride always seemed like an eternity. As I sat there, my father would fall asleep and I would watch all the people get on and off.

We set out to buy the freshest vegetables at the cheapest prices. Being young, I didn't quite understand why a bargain was so important, but now that I'm a big shopper, it's quite exhilarating to buy spinach for twenty-nine cents a pound. We'd buy dried squid, red pepper flakes and the honey sesame candy that we would eat on the way home.

I remember the streets always smelled of dampness, fresh fish and fried dumplings. The sidewalks would be filled with people, just like us, scouting the stores, buying the food we couldn't buy at the supermarket. They looked just like us, the same small Asian families, but it seemed odd that these people who looked similar had to communicate with my father in broken English and body language. They seemed familiar, but at the same time, they were strangers.

We stopped at various produce stands and always ended up with bushels of vegetables, crammed in red plastic bags. It looked as though the plastic rims were sprouting lush green gardens.

When the mornings became hot and sticky, it seemed as though twice as many people came out to hound the shops. I would be smushed in the crush, as everyone paused to gaze at the food stands. I would grab hold for my father's free pinky, which was the perfect size for my hand, and cling to my sister.

Then somewhere on the sidewalk, I'd spot the Carvel store, which seemed like a safe haven. With all my might, I would pray we would go by the shop, just to get a peek inside, or maybe be blessed with a sugar cone topped with a piece of cool delicious heaven. I would try to bring my father around there and relay telepathic messages. If we didn't go near it, my day was ruined and I would curse all the kids in there for eating my ice cream. If it were a truly great day, my father would make his way to the shop. He would open the door, and I could smell the combination of sweet ice cream and the airy refrigerator fumes. I would feel the cool chill, hear the hum of the machines and see the thin Chinese man with the paper hat behind the triangular glass counter. My father usually ordered, but when he gave me the honor, I would be in pure bliss. Sometimes he'd bend down and take a lick, which I didn't mind because it seemed like he was having fun, too.

The last time I was in Chinatown with my father was six years ago. I noticed my Carvel store wasn't there; it had been replaced by a bank. Maybe it was around that time I started fighting with him, or maybe it was when I stopped holding his hand. My life with him seems to be held together with safety pins and bandages to cover up hurtful words and suffering feelings. Now, we exchange simple greetings and quick phrases. We live in separate worlds. I'm trying to move on, and he is trying to relive the past.

My store is gone, just like so many things in life that are said and done and others in life that are left unsaid and undone. Perhaps these are my fondest memories, or maybe they have yet to happen. Maybe the uncomfortable silences and polite smiles will cease, or perhaps it's just a cross I'll have to bear during my life with him. Or maybe there is another Carvel store out there I have yet to discover. ▣

Lenox, Massachusetts

by Patrick Lane

I am driving through the towns of my childhood summers after a college visit. Dad sits in the passenger seat, his body tense against the unpredictability of my hands and feet, the only appendages between us and the sweet hereafter. Mom and Stephie are in the back, straining to peer over my shoulder at these same scenes they remember differently. One town is filled with Saabs and Volvos, a summer retreat for the New York City crowd. The next exudes the dilapidated charm of a communal soul that seeks its sustenance not from green bills but from the green hills that pulse the life beat of this Berkshire clime.

Climb we do—up the faux mountains and down again. I gain momentum from the downward turns and hit the hills at lightning speed. Well, at least fast enough for Mom to murmur, "You're not giving us much confidence, Patrick." But these hills know nothing of confidence nor lack thereof, only a tacit, self-accepting willingness to exist.

I have often thought of these marvelous, mellow mountains during forays through Wordsworth's "lonely rooms" and "hours of weakness," but also when reckless and feckless abandon purges my heart of desire for experience, success, concern. It is then that I yearn for those carefree days of shared adventure when I ran through the woods. Down the sloping dirt road I'd go, its ruts echoing with the creak of horse-drawn carriages, past the sentry house and stables, over the thirsty brook, to Edith Wharton's old mansion, The Mount.

I bounded through these evenings with other children of actors, directors, stage managers. Playing kickball and Frisbee, swimming and fishing in the pond behind our ramshackle boarding house were all reserved for day-light. But the magic dwelt in dusk, slipping into the air as I slipped down to the old white mansion, with its huge, open, wrought-iron gate and high garden walls. The white marble chips of the driveway beneath our feet and the smell of hot chocolate wafting through the air instilled in us a quiet reverence for a magic we could not quite comprehend: the magic of music and dancing, of song and age-old verse.

The set was woven with trees—hardwood and conifer—and I often wandered its warm wooden platforms and hidden backstage dugouts alone. The stage grew out of the fragrant earth, so it was only natural when an actor materialized from the dark forest to add life to its vibrant aura. And so one drifted out upon the sacred Shakes-pearean stage to the music riding the cool summer breeze. This was no ordinary melody, enveloping the audience members reclining in their lawn chairs with haunting winds and mystical chimes. The harmonies rang clear through the night, and as from a dream, the lost sailor emerged from soupy blackness.

Such were those days, standing on the edge of Edith

Wharton's balcony, gazing over the enraptured audience to see my father and friends speaking a foreign, yet familiar, tongue. But what of this do I see now, driving past childhood memories with my father beside and mother and sister behind me?

"Turn in here," he says, as they peer eagerly at same scenes and different memories. We pull into the long dirt driveway that runs past the sentry house, stables and brook, a mile down to the main stage. But it is changed. Ahead, the ruts are widened. They gape open, swallowing airy dreams of past adventures. The road is closed. The theater company has moved.

"Okay, turn around," says Dad.

"Why don't we park here and walk down to the mansion?" I offer.

But Dad replies, "No, Patrick, turn around. We'll go see how the new location is coming. Let's go."

I want to scream, *Don't you understand? We're not here to see the new location. We're here to revisit old memories, to suck in the air of fond remembrance in one deep breath and never let it out.*

But I don't. I have a sinking feeling that the gulp of enchanted air will not be as sweet or eternal as I envision. Reluctantly, I turn the car around and push the soundtrack of *Twelfth Night* into the cassette player. ▣

I Am Ten Years Late

by Ranika Sanchez

I am ten years late.
She is my grandmother,
But did not raise my father.

I am ten years late.
She is my sister, by my father,
But she can never look
Me in the eyes.

I am ten years late.
They are my cousins.
I pretend to smile and make them
Believe I feel comfort in
Being with them.

I am ten years late.
And now my grandmother
Smiles to see her grandchildren.
My sister is grateful to be a family, for once.
My cousins are just happy to be here, but me,
I am too late to understand.

I am ten years late.
I look at these strangers with
Eyes, lips and noses just like mine
They talk about closing the gap in the family.
They talk about becoming a family now,
Which is left up to my generation because
We are young.

Suddenly, I am thinking my mother
Had me right on time because
I can feel the warmth from my family
As we sit at the round table staring in silence.
Then something touches my soul
Where all my emotions are trapped, and a tear
Slowly rolls down my smooth skin.
As it hits my shirt, I wipe the damp spot with
My hand and realize that the only way I can help
Close the family gap is to let my heart loose and
Catch up on time.

Close-Ups:
Revisiting Our Memories

Photo by Nicholas Ruggiero

My Mother and Winnie-the-Pooh

by Kathy Hufford

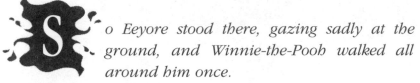

o Eyore stood there, gazing sadly at the ground, and Winnie-the-Pooh walked all around him once.

"Why, what's happened to your tail?" he said in surprise.

"What has happened to it?" said Eeyore.

"It isn't there!"

"Are you sure?"

"Well, either a tail is there or it isn't there. You can't make a mistake about it. And yours isn't there!"

Pooh and Eeyore were speculating about what had happened to the donkey's tail when a high-pitched scream pierced the air. The awful moaning outside my bedroom window sounded like a crazed banshee. I felt my mother's chest convulse as she took a sharp breath.

I suddenly became aware of the pouring rain, the vicious lightning and thunder, and the shrieking winds. The screech of the tornado siren continued to rise and fall slowly, never completing the first scream before beginning its cycle again. With each horrifying note, I was filled with more fear, the almost hypnotic terror that only a young child can experience when faced with the dreaded unknown.

Swinging open the bedroom door, my father burst into the room. "There's a tornado warning," he said, his face tight and pinched. "Hurry, everyone needs to get into the bathroom. It's the only room in the house without windows. Bring anything you need because we might be in there for a while."

Still clutching my *Winnie-the-Pooh* book, I followed my mother around our house and helped gather necessary supplies. As my family piled into the bathroom and sat on the floor, the lights flickered and then went out. I whimpered softly. The tiles on the floor felt like ice against my legs, while the air in the room was hot and musty. It seemed like the walls were closing in, and I could not breathe.

My father quickly clicked on one of the flashlights, and I slowly inspected the faces of my family. I watched my father's jaw clench repeatedly. The weather service predicted that the tornado would not touch down, but he was worried just the same. My mother flashed us a reassuring smile as she covered me and my sister with blankets. My twelve-year-old sister crossed her eyes and stuck out her tongue in my direction.

Winnie-the-Pooh and Eeyore and all their friends had disappeared. I was back in reality. I was a very small, almost insignificant kid scared out of her mind. I had lost any courage I had mustered. I could see the lightning when I closed my eyes. I could hear the thunder when I covered my ears. The wails of the tornado siren echoed in my head. I did the only thing a very small kid could do in that situation: I clutched my blanket tightly, curled myself into a little ball and started to sob.

With a soft click of her tongue, my mom pulled me into her sturdy arms and held me tightly, much like a mother hen protecting her chicks. I inhaled the smell of her cotton nightgown and, for some reason, felt less afraid. My mother began to read, and the pleasant hum of her voice filled my head, overpowering the terrifying wind and rain.

Pooh felt that he ought to say something helpful about the missing tail, but didn't quite know what. So he decided to do something helpful instead.

"Eeyore," he said solemnly, "I, Winnie-the-Pooh, will find your tail for you."

The storm continued far into the night, but I began to focus more on the rise and fall of my mother's voice than on the shrill notes of the sirens. I was pulled back into the story, and into the next story, and the next. Then, I fell into a deep sleep.

Whenever a storm enters my life, I reach for my *Winnie-the-Pooh* book.

Whenever I feel lonely or afraid, the familiar stories comfort me like an old friend. I identify most with Eeyore and his lost tail. It may bring a tear to my eye, but it continues to remind me that my mother will always be there for me. I continue to recall that she, and a little imagination, helped me conquer one of my greatest fears. Courage was my lost tail, and thanks to my mother and Winnie-the-Pooh, I found it. ▣

Shifting Sand

by Joe Haynes

After I spent an hour looking toward the horizon over the serene blue glass, I saw yesterday's birthday boy looking like a million bucks, dark circles under half-open eyes, old hat over uncombed hair coming down the stairs. I knew our swim would be the closest thing he had to a shower that morning.

It was 9:00 A.M. on August twenty-third. The night before, my best friend turned eighteen and we had celebrated. That night my eyelids did not close except to blink, so I wandered down to the beach to unwind. I tried in vain to hold onto the night that had already succumbed to the rising sun, and tried to grasp a few moments of the quickly fleeting summer that was already giving way to autumn-painted leaves.

Though we looked terrible and felt even worse, we smiled at each other's sight, remembering last night's fun. One part of him was asleep and the other dead as he slowly sauntered through the crowd across the sand toward me. He parked himself and his old rainbow-striped chair beside me, just as he had every summer for over a decade. He clumsily crashed into the low seat, simultaneously letting out an exhausted groan, and violently reclining his chair until it was parallel with the scorching sand. I do not know if he fell asleep, but he did fall silent until the great sphere was at its highest on the ceiling of our cloudless blue tent.

All the while I silently sat and watched two young boys run and jump into the blue-green sheet which, to my surprise, did not break or crack, but rather seemed to swallow, ingest and then happily regurgitate them.

The two boys seemed surrounded by an air of contentment as they played, just as I was surrounded by the sweltering heat and bright sunlight. I sat for what seemed like an eternity, envying those carefree boys. They reminded me of a forgotten era when I played with the seemingly dead kid beside me 'til the sun reluctantly hid behind the inn. We played every game you could think of, and some only the combined imaginations of boys seven and eight years old could dream up. We rode waves that now pass just above our knees, failed every day at digging to China and ran home to catch our favorite TV shows.

As I sat watching how happy those boys were at play, I wanted nothing more than to be their age again just for one day, even one hour. It seemed time was laughing at its domination over my life. There were reminders everywhere of time's ever-shifting sands, its always-turning tides. Just yesterday my friend blew out eighteen candles; I remember getting yelled at for sticking my finger in the frosting that had held only eight burning shafts of wax.

Realizing Apollo was still rapidly riding his golden chariot across the sky, I roused the unconscious mess at my side. And just like the two boys, we recklessly ran toward the water, kicking sand on people's towels, and dove together into the comfortably cold Atlantic Ocean.

I felt as if I was diving back into my distant past. Before surfacing I held my breath for an extra moment, sensing that in the water I had actually beaten time. I expected to be greeted by a chubby, missing-toothed, wiffle-headed boy. I surfaced with wide eyes, but to my dismay all I found different about the young man off to college in three days was that he was a little less groggy now.

Once again time triumphed over me, but because of that transitory moment when I held my breath, I know someday I will conquer time. And the sun will rise in the west and set in the east, and all the lost days that have fallen behind me will be laid new in front of my unbelieving eyes. And I will recapture my past. ▣

After-Bath Powders

by Ashley Crawford

Sitting alone in the dreary room
Waiting as time crawled sluggishly along
  for news; good or bad
The unpleasant smell of sickness and medicines
Forced my mind to flee .
Sounds of my own laughter rang in my ears
As memories forced my face into a glowing grin
Soap bubbles clung softly to my baby skin
Their strawberry scent sneaking up to tickle my nose
My grandma, now younger, stronger, healthier
Lifts me up
The water rolls down my body, trickling back into
  the bubbles with a soft, soothing fizz
Now wrapped in a fuzzy towel
Her arms embraced me in a loving hug as she led me
  to her large, comforting bed
I giggled in pure delight when she removed the small,
  white can from her pink, flowered housecoat
White powder floated up once it was opened
  filling the air and our noses with the sweet, light scent
Smiling, she gently patted my slightly wet skin
With the powerful powder puff
Until I was coated with white, snowlike flakes

Dressed and once again embraced
I was allowed to skip and play
  go on my merry way
Voices broke the rolling film of memories
Once more I return to the harshness of reality
Rising to my feet I walk through the dreadful halls
Into the hospital room filled with illness
Older and more appreciative, I make my way to her
Embracing her fragile body
With the love she'd given me
So many times in years before
During my after-bath powders.

Photo by Rachel Cohen

This Was Mine

by Jamie L. Heberling

Lately, time has zipped by as quickly as a swatted, pesky fly. But it hasn't always gone that fast. I used to enjoy the long, careless days of childhood.

I would stay out until dusk with the neighborhood gang, playing kick-the-can. The autumn sun would turn the entire sky a dreamy pink and the light would reflect off the leaves. The smell of burning twigs, leaves and old newspapers lingered in the heavy air. The chill would cause my hair to stand on end. At the sound of my mom's whistle, my sister and I would head for home. I would tumble into the house with grass-stained knees and elbows.

This was my childhood.

On steamy summer Sunday mornings, my sister, my dad and I would trek to the nearby reservoir. My sister and I, dressed in our best fishing apparel, would juggle our fishing poles and tackle boxes until we got to the rocks where we would finally set them down.

"This is the best bluegill spot we're gonna find. You girls want to fish for bluegills, don't you? 'Cause if you wanna go for the catfish, we've gotta walk all the way 'round to the other side," Dad said.

"This is fine, Dad," we said. We didn't care what we fished for. Besides, it would have taken too much energy to go to the other side. We fished all day with the sun's heat radiating off our backs and time didn't mean a thing.

This was my childhood.

An old, widowed woman named Mrs. Newberger used to live in a brick house beside us. Her backyard emulated *The Secret Garden*. It was filled with colorful flowers, bushes and exotic shrubbery that bloomed when the sun shone and closed when the sun hid behind the clouds. Amazingly, despite Alzheimer's, Mrs. Newberger knew the genus and species of every plant. She never knew my name. Sometimes I would sneak into her garden and pick a flower for my mother. Once, instead of just clipping the stem, I accidentally uprooted the whole plant. I held the dirty plant in my hand, not knowing what to do. Even though Mrs. Newberger's eyesight was failing and she normally couldn't pick out the broad side of a barn, she caught me red-handed. Terrified, I dropped the plant and ran home, forgetting about my mother's gift.

This was my childhood.

If only I could be seven years old and scared of Mrs. Newberger again, things would be okay. If only I could be watching the bob from my fishing pole go up and down, time wouldn't mean a thing. If only I could play kick-the-can in the autumn breeze, my childhood would come back. If only I were only there again, I wouldn't wish away the years like a pesky fly. 🔲

Marc

by Tiffany Gump

I remember my carefree life in the purple storybook house on Maple Street. I remember climbing tall, forbidding trees, huge red ants, sweet, flaky, fresh blackberry pies and wagon rides down the hills and through the cemetery. I remember my friends, my family, my pets. But more than anything, I remember Marc.

Everyone on Maple Street knew and loathed Marc. He was a holy terror. His short buzzed hair, chubby middle and burly arms were the fiercest I had encountered in all my years. The little brat spilled whitewash on my frilly, flowered Sunday dress on purpose! That was right before I punched him in the eye, for which I was grounded for a whole week. He shot sticks at my bike while I was riding it, wedging them in the spokes and causing me to crash into the neighbor's fence. He trashed our campsites, stole our toys and annoyed every kid and adult on Maple Street.

So one cheerful summer morning we decided to get revenge for everything he had ever done to my brother, sister and me. First, we rallied the neighborhood kids and huddled together to decide just what to do. We held nothing back from our plot; nothing was too bold, bad or disgusting. He deserved everything. We got a bucket and filled it with mud and slimy pond water from behind the bushes in cranky old man Dino's garden. Whatever we could find, we mixed into the bucket: squishy frog guts, moldy maple syrup, slimy pancake mix and, my contribution, lovely fresh skunk innards from up the road, just to name a few. Then, while we girls got crab apples to throw at Marc (the wormiest, slimiest, squishiest we could find), the boys stayed behind and mixed the evil brew in the plastic cauldron.

Now, our last challenge was to get Marc outside. Lucky me, a rather unfair committee of my peers volunteered me. I stumbled up to his front porch, scared stiff, with whispered choruses of "Go! You're almost at the porch!" behind me. Marc's threatening house loomed as I held as many blackberries as a seven-year-old could carry in her pudgy fist.

With a sweaty, shaking hand I rang the doorbell. He answered my beckon of doom, looming over me like a terrible stone demon statue with a look of cold hate frozen on his scarred face that made my bones rattle. I hesitated, unsure of whether to risk getting beaten up or run away and put up with being labeled a coward—the kid who ran away from freedom—for the rest of my existence. I just couldn't let the others down. I mustered all my pride and smashed the blackberries on Marc's ugly punk face, then raced frantically toward the safe haven behind the fence of freedom with Marc in hot pursuit.

It seemed as if all hell had broken loose and was singeing my tennis shoes, chasing me with unspeakable horrors and motivating me to run with all my strength lest I be doomed to an eternity of Marc-ish nightmares.

I changed my course just as I had lured him close enough to the fence and dove into the street with barely enough time to look back. The others stood up, hauling the bucket that seemed to be bubbling with anxiety and *splooooosh!* They hit him dead on! He was covered from head to toe with the putrid, slimy water. The look of sheer surprise and humiliation on his face was way better than any reward anyone could have given us for this courageous feat. Marc stepped forward, threatening to tear us to shreds, but coming from a four-foot puke pile, that didn't scare us much. I guess he realized he was powerless, and turned and ran crying—crying—inside to tattle to his mommy. She was not amused by our light-hearted fun, and Marc's dad came outside and sicced their evil, ugly dog on us.

We scattered in all directions, running down Maple Street as fast as our feet could carry us. Then the massive beast caught hold of my brother. I didn't stick around to find out what happened after Marc's dad got to him, but I didn't really have to. Cory showed up later, with Marc's dad, at our house. The biggest bit of trouble was yet to come: Mom, and all the terrors and threats that only a mother could possess. Marc's dad told her the whole story, and she thanked him, then shut the door and watched him stagger up the street.

As she turned to us, a broad smile spread across her face. She laughed. We laughed. I guess she despised Marc as much as we did. We only got grounded for a week, which isn't too bad considering the extent of our crime. That was my ultimate kid moment. The few seconds of impact and the confused look on Marc's face will live in my memory forever. ▣

Wedding Pictures

by Joanne Wang

I'm short. When I am no smart, I have nothing special." I knew my mother was relaying her few words of wisdom, but I kept my eyes on the supermarket meatball she had put on my dinner plate.

"Your dad love his college. He find out that he like research. I have bad college. I did not find what I like. I still do not know." Searching for her tears, I raised my eyes from the meatball to hers. She smiled.

As I cut my meatball into thin slices, I could only focus on all the mistakes in her grammar. I was not ready for one of the mother-daughter chats I once desired.

"But like I say yesterday, I look back and I have good life. God bless me so many ways. I should not feel bad. I just feel like I didn't do anything," she smiled again.

My eyes moved to the bowl of tortellini between us. It was filled with spaghetti sauce, meatballs and green peas. It looked like a repulsive combination of leftovers, which is exactly what it was. Next to the bowl, the gray pot of rice seemed out of place. My mother viewed rice as a staple: A meal was not complete without vegetables, fruit and rice. On her plate, the rice was mixed right in with the tortellini concoction.

The silence that normally characterized dinner without Dad resumed. Seven-minute dinner, plate in sink, homework time. I glanced at the clock and prepared for my retreat. But before I could move, my mother decided to impart more of her ungrammatical knowledge.

"My sister, the one who . . ." my mother looked as if she wouldn't be able to say the word "died." I nodded.

"She was so pretty." Impatience began to rise and I rolled my eyes. Couldn't she think of anything to say besides the fact that her sister was pretty? Physical appearances are not that important. She said the same thing last year when my cousin died of heart problems.

"She died of drug. We didn't really have drug like now. She sniff, what you say, something like glue," she said, more to herself than to me.

"No kidding?" I had always thought she died of some disease.

I looked at my mother again: her white shirt, short hair, plastic glasses. I saw her often, talked with her less. She had told me little about her life. Well, I had never asked. I had viewed her as the person I would never become. I never bothered to find out why she had gone from the top of her class at college and a woman on top of the world to one who spent a lifetime cooking meatballs and cleaning the kitchen floor. My curiosity about her had grown. Perhaps I was searching for an explanation for her depression. Perhaps I was frightened because I was slowly learning I was more like my mother than I'd ever imagined.

After leaving my plate in the sink, I went upstairs and pulled out a photo album from underneath the road maps and old Bibles. The cover was stamped with orange and brown flowers, the binding undone. Although I could not recall looking through it, I knew it was their wedding pictures.

I laughed. There was Dad, skinny as ever with the same mocking expression. And there was my mother. She was wearing a strapless yellow dress and platform shoes. She was smiling, but with an expression I had never seen. It had spirit.

"Am I pretty?" My mother stood behind me. She was. I nodded. "I told you. See? I was pretty."

She pointed to a close-up of her face. "I really not that pretty. I had one of the best makeup person in the country. See? I ask for light makeup. At that time, most people wear dark. You see how light that is; looks natural." She pointed to the yellow dress picture. "I look more like that." I said nothing. I thought she looked much prettier in the yellow dress picture.

"You should know my family," she said.

I was much closer to my father's side and knew only one of my mother's sisters. She had given me the stuffed-to-ripping Hello Kitty wallet I carried around to the dismay of my more sophisticated friends.

"This is Grandma."

My grandma seemed so different from the person who called once in a while for my mother. I hadn't seen her in eight years, and there were no pictures of her on our walls. Grandma looked chubbier and less fragile than I had imagined.

"Grandpa." I remembered him even less. I recently learned he had divorced my grandma. Though he seemed like the bad guy of the family, my mother sympathized with him.

"How old were you when they got divorced?" I asked.

"I had just come to America." My mother came here after college; I figured her parents had divorced when they were about sixty.

My mother pointed to her sister (the one who gave me the wallet) and her brother. Then, she pointed to a girl in a blue plaid dress with straight hair that fell just above her mouth. She must have been about thirteen. I stared at the girl—it had to be the youngest sister, the one who died at nineteen. I'd spent one summer with her daughter, who had been adopted by one of the other faces in the picture. A whole summer, and I just passed her by as some relative. I wondered if my brother had ever asked about my mother's sister. Was he as oblivious as I?

The last page had four pictures, but my eyes were drawn to a dark one in the bottom left corner. My father and mother stood with glasses of wine. My mother was laughing. Around her neck was a Victorian choker.

My throat tightened, and I couldn't hear a word my mother was saying. I kept staring at the choker—its dark velvet, ivory stone, rose bead. It was the same choker my mother had kept for twenty-five years. It was the same choker I had taken out of her drawer, unaware of its history. It was the same choker I had lost one day, and never found.

"And that's the pictures," I heard my mother say. I smiled at her. When words fail, I have learned to smile.

"Goody, goody?" my mother asked.

"Goody, goody," I replied.

I watched my mom leave the room. And then, staring at that lost choker, I began to cry. ▣

Rhubarb and Paper Towels

by Erica Hebert

At my grandma's home, in the dead of summer, everything was served on Bounty paper towels. Dropped off by our parents on their way to work in the early morning, my cousins, my sister and I would embark on great outdoor adventures that could only take place during lazy summer days, and only in Grandma's great backyard. I remember gathering around her coffee table, our dirty and scraped knees drawn beneath us, and munching on sticky PB&J sandwiches. They always tasted better when served on paper towels.

During the summer, we could be anything we wanted to be. We were wolves, with names like "Sharp Fang" or "White Foot," the kind of names that could only be found in the sappiest of Disney movies. Then we were Indians, picking random leaves and plants, probably poisonous, and mashing them into salves. We were always barefoot, climbing trees like little heathens and using sharp stones to whittle twigs into great spears. Then my grandmother would call us in for lunch, and we came from our expeditions, hungry and tanned, to eat our daily bread. Served on a paper towel, of course.

We never thought of my grandmother as old, but, as the years wore on, her age was a brutal fact we would rather overlook. I remember how she put on her lipstick. I would sit on the toilet, basking in the glow of the vanity light and watch as she traced her lips with magnificent colors. First the top lip, careful to stay within the lines, then, with a great sweep, her bottom lip. A quick press of a bit of tissue, and she was done. I would gaze at her perfectly colored lips, then at the discarded tissue, which still held a flawless imprint. When I grew up, I would put on my lipstick just as she had.

My grandmother also had a garden, fenced in and charted on our maps of make-believe as a vast no-man's-land. Although she grew only a few plants, it was like nothing we had ever seen. To our small eyes, the garden, which we eventually developed the courage to venture into, was a microcosm of wild grapes, huge blueberry bushes, and, best of all, hidden rhubarb plants.

Exhausted and famished from our great adventures, but with a couple hours left before lunchtime, the bravest would sneak into Grandma's garden and snatch up a bunch of grapes or a handful of the biggest blueberries. Then we would scamper off to our favorite climbing tree and share the forbidden fruit. Believe me, those wild grapes, with the skin so tough that it had to be spit out, tasted better than countless exotic fruits.

The rhubarb, however, was another story. Some days, after lunch when we were resting in front of the fan, my grandmother would stroll out to her garden with a pair of scissors and return with three of the largest rhubarb stalks. We would pretend not to notice, but then we would just happen to appear in the kitchen, where she would cut the fruit up into little pieces, and we would reap the bounty. This is not to say that we were so deprived that we found great enjoyment from a stalk of rhubarb, but we couldn't help but discover simple pleasures in those summer days at my grandmother's home.

My grandmother made everything just right. I now look back fondly on my scarred knees and elbows, old battle wounds from tree branches and pricker bushes of summer days gone by. Everything was so simple at my grandmother's home. I remember summer days, so hot and bright that they remain like the flash of a camera in my mind. I've been shaped by my grandmother, with her beautiful backyard, amazing climbing trees, ripe rhubarb and meals served on paper towels. ▣

Photo by Stephen Siperstein

Concrete Promises

by Jordana Mishory

multi-colored blurs whir by
our tan-speckled sidewalk,
their wheels pounding out a rhythm reminiscent of
scurrying ants stumbling beneath the weight
*   of the universe,*
ignoring the occasional chubby finger thrust
*   in their paths*
en route to their colony.
exhaust fumes and daisies and newly mowed grass
perfume the sun-kissed afternoon.
the elderly farmhouse relaxes in the shadows—
the off-white-stuccoed guardian protecting us
*   from the uncertainty*
of tomorrow.
connected by concrete promises, we sat there,
two girls with silver shiny braces and brown curly hair
sitting each in our own square . . .
matching navy-blue school bags tossed aside,
the grocery-bag-covered books contained in them
*   a memory*
of yesterday.
the green overgrown bush tickles the sidewalk,
as we erupt in a flurry of giggles.
sharing the secrets
of today.

Snow Day

by Jessica Griffin

I pressed my face against the window where fat snowflakes fell into the white blanket of snow already covering the ground. I sighed and the window fogged under my hot breath. I hated snow, especially when it was only a matter of time before I had to go out in it. It never failed. Every time I went out during a snowstorm, I always managed to slip on a piece of ice, and get my socks soaking wet.

"Time for school," my babysitter, Ann, bellowed, verifying my fears. I had to go outside.

Her son, Andy, bounded up the stairs to me and threw on his winter jacket. Wearily I stood, wiping the fog from the window with my fingertip. I found my winter clothes and pulled on my ratty pink snow pants, purple coat, gloves, hat and boots.

Andy shouted to hurry. He was standing anxiously at the front door, his hand twisting the knob. When I got there, he pulled the door open with all his might, letting in a burst of air. Then he flew out, running across the snow, screaming with delight. I chased after him, my heavy boots weighing down my feet. I heard Ann shout after us, but I wasn't sure what she said. Probably something like "shut the door," because seconds later it slammed so loudly that it echoed across the yard. Looking back, I started off after Andy.

He was sitting at the bottom of the driveway, waiting impatiently.

"I don't want to go to school that bad," I pouted.

I suppose he agreed because he slowed to a walk. He stuck out his tongue and caught a few flakes.

"I love the snow," he stated simply.

I hated the snow. All I could think was how numb my toes were, how I'd have to get on the smelly bus and sit with wet pants, and that Mrs. Read was giving us a spelling test today. I would have much preferred being inside where it was warm, drinking hot chocolate and watching television.

"Hey guys," someone squealed behind us. Jennifer, our friend from across the street, was several steps behind us. She was a whirl of curly brown hair and smelled of Winterfresh gum and her father's cigars.

"Jess, I forgot my spelling list," she said, her big brown eyes wide. "How do you spell 'picture'? I can never remember that one."

"P-I-C-H-E-R," Andy sighed as though it were the easiest thing in the world.

"That's *not* how you spell it," I said.

"Yeah-huh," he retorted.

"Nope." I stuck my hands into my pocket and balled them into fists, trying to warm my frostbitten fingers.

We approached the bus stop that was actually just a bend in the road. Today there were snowbanks obstructing our view. Although the plow had come, the roads were already covered with snow and slick ice. Andy immediately discarded his bag and climbed to the top.

"I'm king of the mountain!" he shouted, thrusting his fists into the air. Jennifer and I looked at each other and rolled our eyes. Boys were so silly.

"The bus is going to come any second," Jennifer said, pulling up her jacket sleeve to reveal a lime green plastic watch. "The bus driver will let you have it if she sees you up there. Come down."

Andy frowned, but slid down. And we stood there, the bitter winds whipping against us. My lips were raw and cracked. Jennifer's nose was running. And we waited, and waited, and waited.

When forever seemed to have come and gone, Andy began to dig tunnels into the snow bank. The snow had stopped, but the dreary overcast skies threatened additional downpours. A lone car passed, but no school bus.

"We should go back," I said anxiously. My whole body shook from the cold. My ears were so numb I couldn't feel them.

"What if the bus comes after we leave?" Jennifer asked, peering down the empty road, hoping to see the bus coming around the corner.

"Ann will drive us," I said, more confidently than I felt.

"No, she won't." Andy met my gaze. His green eyes burned into me. "My mom won't drive us, and we'll never get there."

They looked at each other and then at me. This was a desirable outcome. Missing the bus meant missing school, and missing Mrs. Read's spelling test. But we feared the wrath of Ann who had a horrid temper. This seemed too simple, and the burden of ditching class was too much for seven-year-olds like us. Still, there was no bus, and it was cold.

Andy grabbed a heap of snow in his gloved hand and challenged us to a snowball fight. But we were too cold.

I'm not sure what persuaded us to head home, but seconds later I was chasing Andy up the slippery driveway toward Ann's house. Flurries of snow began again.

Andy opened the door without waiting to see if I was behind him. A thick wall of heat burst from inside. It felt so good that I didn't hesitate to run in. The door blew shut behind us.

"What are you guys still doing here?" Ann demanded, standing at the top of the stairs. She held a vacuum cleaner hose against her hip. Her thick black hair was pulled back in a bright red bandanna. I found myself staring in fear that if I met her gaze she'd start to scream.

"The bus never came," Andy explained.

Ann looked at her watch in horror. "You guys have been outside for an hour?" she cursed under her breath. "Damn school. Well, come in, take off your boots. I just vacuumed. I'm gonna call them and see what's going on."

We did as we were told and sat side-by-side on the couch. I didn't want to take off my coat in case Ann made us go back out and wait for the bus. We sat in silence, waiting and listening to her on the phone. Her voice was tense, and at one point I thought she might cry.

"I told you, I can't drive them; my car is broken. Jessica isn't my daughter. Her mom will kill me if I can't get her to school," she paused for a long time, and then sighed, "Okay, all right, good-bye."

When she walked into the living room, our eyes were

trained on her. She grabbed the vacuum cleaner and frowned at us.

"The bus couldn't get up this way, so you guys have the day off from school."

Andy and I both screamed enthusiastically. We were off the couch like a shot, throwing our snow boots back on.

No school, no test. I ran out into the yard and rolled around in the snow, the cold not bothering me anymore. I couldn't wait to see all my friends and brag to them about how I got the day off from school. Andy pounced on top of me, landing hard on my ribs, but I didn't feel it. Both of us were shouting in happiness. In the distance I saw Jennifer running toward us. I loved the snow. ▣

King of the Mountain

by Janna Jae Wilber

The idea hit us as we stared out into the distance. Simultaneously, we turned to each other, grinned and started running toward the gigantic rock. The wind rushed at our hair, nipping our necks. I lost my shoes somewhere on the way to the overgrown field. Running as fast as we could through the mist, we had only one thought on our minds: to be king of the mountain. A childish idea at fourteen, for sure, but in a time of failing friendships and state tests, if we could only break free for a moment, vitality would return to our souls.

Around the shrubs we leapt, stomping on strawberries that lay in our path. I felt as free as the birds chirping loudly at the beautiful sight of mountains, lakes and trees. As we neared our destination, we saw it wasn't just the obstacle of climbing the enormous rock that we had to overcome, but getting to the rock, which was actually in the water. We came to the edge of the lake and the rock seemed miles away, though it was only twenty feet. It was barely June and the water was chilly on this breezy, sunless day, but it only took a millisecond to realize what we had to do. With pure delight, we raced into the frigid water, stopping after a few feet to shiver and let the true absurdity of the act sink in, just as the ice water was sinking into our once dry, warm clothes.

Life can be so overwhelming sometimes that we try to run and ignore it all. Yet as I swam toward the rock, my outlook changed and I saw existence as not just the little world I was living in, but the big picture, full of open areas and opportunity—a place where we all rely on each other. I was swimming as a solution to my stress.

Within minutes, we had reached the great rock and faced yet another setback: algae. It made the rock slippery and nearly impossible to get both feet on. This obstacle could slow us no more than the fifty-eight-degree water had. Laura was on top of the rock in no time, lending a hand to pull me up. At last we had made it. The wind whipped hard against our cold bodies that were weighted with water. Goose bumps rose high on our skin, trying to keep in some heat. Nevertheless, I felt only triumph looking out on the water. At that moment, I was the king of the world; even the fast-paced waves splashing against the rock below couldn't reach me.

I cherish the moment when I stood on that tremendous rock looking at the mountains that stretched around us covered with dark mounds of clouds. In the bigger picture of my life, I had friendships in an uproar and finals approaching, but in that moment, everything was perfectly peaceful and full of sparkle. I jumped into that icy water to learn what I could do and, with that, became less apprehensive. I had lived for the moment. ▣

Carbondale

by Holly Miller

Off that dirt road
to the old farmhouse
where Trouble always waited for me
in the barn,
and Grandpa was forever swearing
at the horses, and swatting them
with that broken tree branch.
Where that murky swamp
was the backyard
and the secrets lay engulfed in
that tipsy wooden canoe
but I wouldn't go near them,
for fear of the
mystical mud.
And it was always crisply cool
at night
even in the summer.
So we'd take those night walks
under clear blue skies,
fastened back with glittering diamonds
that twinkled, like Grandpa's eyes
when he told stories
of the war, the CIA and Colorado.

I would sit, entranced,
curiosity the strongest emotion
of a young child.
Blissfully unaware that it would be
the last time
I would see the sparkle of his eyes
reflecting the rolling countryside.

Photo by Jessica Hootnick

The Big Pool

by Katelyn M. Smith

ooking back on my childhood, I was no joy to raise. I was one of those kids they make *Problem Child* movies about. My mother aged twenty-five years during the first five of my life. I was a real pill.

At age three, I developed this uncanny ability to evaporate into thin air whenever I found myself in a busy public place. I ran off in malls, supermarkets, parades and fairs; I disappeared in places at the worst possible times.

My best disappearing act occurred when I was three at our city's pool. At seventeen, I have yet to live this stunt down. The neighborhood pool is the largest pool east of the Mississippi. Any given summer day, roughly a thousand happy swimmers can be found splashing around in its overly chlorinated water.

My mother knew me well enough not to take me to the pool on a regular basis. But there was one day it was just too hot to stay home. My mother figured she could manage my brother and me for two measly hours, so she packed us up and off we went.

My mom underestimated us. My brother, who has the swimming abilities of a cinder block, was doing his best rock impression on the bottom of the pool while my mother frantically tried to help him learn how to stand up in the water. I watched the little spectacle for a while until I decided I was not amused. I looked up the hill and was awestruck by the most gigantic slide I had ever seen. I wanted to ride it and so I did.

It is still a mystery how a three-year-old managed to stroll out the gates of the pool unnoticed. The lifeguards usually stop lone children and send them back to their mothers. My mother's best guess is that I somehow joined a daycare or camp group leaving the pool and left unobserved by the lifeguards.

The next thing I remember is standing at the top of the largest slide ever with my Cabbage Patch doll sitting in front of me. I flew down and was overjoyed by the wind blowing my short bangs off my forehead.

Meanwhile, at the pool, my mother had noticed her daughter was among the missing. She checked my usual hiding spots and could not find me. She assumed that since I was not stashed in a bush or behind a rock, I must have drowned. She informed the lifeguards who evacuated the entire pool and began meticulously combing the pool floor.

I watched the pool evacuation from my perch on the slide. The teenage lifeguards looked like adults to me. I assumed they were having adult swim. I thought how angry the other kids must be that adult swim was lasting so long. Usually it was twenty minutes long. They searched for me for forty-five minutes.

After twenty runs down the slide, I got lonely. I went in search of friends and found myself in a daycare group for six-year-olds. The woman in charge counted her herd of children and discovered she had an extra. It was pretty obvious that I was not a runt six-year-old. She knew right away that I must be the "drowned" girl the pool staff was searching for.

She took my doll in one arm and me in the other and escorted me back to the gates. I was immediately mobbed by the pool staff and dragged back to my mom.

My next recollection is a very silent ride home. I sat in the backseat and wondered why my mother looked so upset. I also wondered why I had to wear a bright orange tag on my bathing suit. I realized when I was older that this was to prevent me from leaving the pool area again.

From that day on, I was one of those kids on a leash. Whenever we went to a crowded place, I wore a bungee cord on my wrist, which considerably inhibited my wandering abilities. No matter how hard I tried, I was never more than four feet from my mother.

It was five years before I was ever taken to that pool again. ◙

Sunday Outings

by Kimberly Burke Reilly

When I was a child, Sunday was a special day. It wasn't a day when the whole family came home for an afternoon turkey dinner. Rather, my parents and I usually ate a hot dog or hamburger at a roadside stand. But, no matter where we ate, our Sunday excursion would take us near the ocean. So every Sunday we would find ourselves driving with no real destination, but in the direction of some small New England town by the sea.

These drives usually occurred in the spring and the fall. The leaves were either a fresh, new green or a brilliant mix of yellow, orange and red. We enjoyed the weather because, for the most part, it was refreshingly crisp, but not cold. The view of the ocean always complemented the feel of the air with rough waves crashing against the sandy beaches and jagged cliff rocks. We knew, because of the time of the year, that the water was cold and it felt cozy to be wearing a warm sweater and an old pair of jeans.

Along the way people were always cleaning out their houses and garages. So, as we drove the winding back roads, there was one yard sale after another. My mom insisted on stopping at every one. But we didn't mind because it gave us time to get out and stretch. My mother was content picking and poking at the various "collectibles." And I was always happy when Mom would get back in the car and hand me one of her great finds, like a book of party games that would keep me occupied for hours.

I came to recognize every bump in the road, too. I would watch the time and know when we were approaching our ride home. My dad always allowed enough time so that we would be back in time for the five o'clock church service. But it wasn't just the time that clued me in to the ride home; it was our route. No matter where we spent most of the day, we would take the long way home by the shore road that I thought was one of the most beautiful. My father would have a smile on his face, knowing that rather than the expressway, he would take us the scenic way where the view was magnificent.

The road was a winding cliff road with clusters of mansions. Each was different, but all shared the amazing ocean view. And the kelly green, well-groomed lawns were a vivid contrast to the blue of the ocean. We could see the wide open Atlantic, rough and scattered with white sails. If it were sunny, the water would be a beautiful deep blue, reflecting the sky, with foamy white caps accenting the puffy white clouds in the sky. And if it were windy, we could sometimes see the spray of the surf wetting the jagged cliff rocks. Occasionally, a mossy rock wall would obstruct the view, but as we drove around the bend, we could once again see the big blue mass that stretched to the horizon. And later, as I sat in my pew at church, I could feel the tightness of my skin and the itchiness of my eyes from the salty ocean air.

It is not often now that we make that Sunday excursion. But whenever I go to the beach on a summer day with my friends, I always drive, because I know the way. And when we sit in the sand, perspiring and covered with oil, I think of another time when the air was not as hot, and a feeling of happiness runs through me, as my heart fills with fond memories. ▣

Photo by Stephen Siperstein

Moon Watching

by Lexie Rich

The swing set had always been my favorite part of our whole yard. My grandfather had built it for my sixth birthday, and when I turned nine, I was still addicted to the natural high of that immaculate moment when I got up there with the birds, always reaching for the clouds but never quite touching them. From far away, I could easily discern the rumbling of a big camp bus that carried my two best friends. Using the rest of my energy, I gave one hard push and jumped off, landing in the soft grass. I skipped past my house and onto the sidewalk as I watched the bus pause just long enough for two kids to get off.

"Nick! Ashley!" I called, my skip turning into a moderate jog. The two stopped, hearing their names. "Are you busy tonight? My father said he would set up the tent if you wanted to stay over. It could be fun."

Nick, Ashley and I had been friends ever since I had moved there. We had shared bottles, toys, friends and enemies, but had remained almost as one—especially when Chris, the neighborhood bully, came around calling me "Ex-Lex." With Nick to my left and Ashley to my right, I was afraid of no one. Our emotions were felt by each, and we could finish each other's sentences. Most important, we had fun. Ashley was humorous, Nick was silly but funny, and I was there just to laugh.

The three of us hung indoors for a while and watched reruns of *Saved by the Bell* until my father got home. We pounced, each pestering him to set up the tent immediately. An hour later the sky was already darkening, and my father had just put in the last spikes to hold it down. Excitedly, we rushed in all at once, almost causing it to collapse. We giggled in the spacious tent. I spread out my dark purple sleeping bag, and Nick and Ashley each laid theirs down. We lay down and stared in silence at the blue top of the tent.

"Wouldn't it be cool if the top had a sunroof?" Nick asked.

"Stupid. Sunroofs let in the suuun," Ashley exaggerated. "If you hadn't noticed, it is currently night, evening, dusk," she explained. I giggled at her sarcasm.

"You know what we could do?" I wondered aloud. "We could tell ghost stories, and maybe make s'mores, like we were really camping out," I proposed.

"I'm pretty hungry," Nick trailed off.

"What else is new?" Ashley retorted.

"Dinner?" I offered, and smiled at how they always fought with simple words. And so we headed inside for dinner.

The next time we came out to the tent it was about eight. I carried a few ghost stories and a flashlight. Nick had stocked up on the snacks for the night, and Ashley trailed behind, gazing at the stars.

"Look at the sky, guys," she told us. "It's a perfect night! It's warm, and look at all the stars! I wonder how many stars live up there."

"They don't live, silly. Stars are just fire."

"I think the stars are diamonds," I suggested.

"Then God must be rich," Ashley joked. I smiled at her comment and continued gazing up, mesmerized by the only source of light from the dark sky.

"Where's the moon?" Nick asked. Ashley and I realized we couldn't find it.

"I know, I bet it got jealous of the stars that brighten up the sky, so it went back into its room," Ashley suggested.

"Or maybe it forgot to do its homework," Nick muttered. Ashley and I laughed. I took one of Nick's arms and re-entered the tent. We each got cozy in our sleeping bags, and Nick started with his own ghost story, which was funnier than scary. We told stories, ate too much chocolate and then played a round of truth or dare. By 11:00 Ashley and Nick were tired.

"Aw, come on guys! It's way too early to go to bed! We can play night tag or catch fireflies. Don't quit now," I urged.

"Be quiet, Lex. You don't have camp tomorrow morning. You get to sleep late," Nick whined.

"Your mother is going to bring us home at 7:00. That's way early. I need my beauty sleep," Ashley said with a humorous smile.

"Suit yourself," I muttered. "I'm taking the flashlight. Good night, you two." I made my way out. I tiptoed to my porch and grabbed a small jar. I skipped along the lush grass, my steps barely making a sound. "Come on, fireflies!" I tried enticing them. "This would be so much easier with three people," I complained ten minutes later, exasperated with my failure to catch even one. I yawned and unsteadily fell backwards onto the grass.

"Whoa," I muttered when my eyes found the moon high above. It looked as big as three beach balls put together, placed in the sky and painted a crisp white. Just the size of the moon seemed to put all the stars out of place and beat their light by a million times. As I stared, it seemed to get brighter and brighter until I couldn't stand it and had to shut my eyes. "Whoa," I repeated. I raised my hand above my head and pretended to write words on the moon, so that the whole world could see my secret, nocturnal message.

Silently someone approached me from behind. I jumped at first, but realizing it was Nick, I smiled and lay back down with him beside me. "Wow," he said softly. I turned to face him, looking at his face hypnotically watching the light that brightened the night sky and the hibernating world below.

Another face appeared beside Nick's, and Ashley took a seat in the middle. She smiled at me, and we all turned our gaze to the moon that seemed to watch us in return. A minute later Ashley asked, "Do you think other friends are watching the moon right now?"

"I hope so," I replied.

"That would be nice," Nick added. For the rest of the night we stared up at the moon, now our good friend. Sometime between then and the time the sun took the moon's place, we all fell asleep, all together, almost as one. ▣

Epilogue

by Brett Elizabeth Larkin

I magine you are on a precarious rope bridge, high above a gorge. You can't go backward; you can only inch forward, and the bridge keeps swaying. That's what it is like to be a teen. You are forbidden to return to the land of simple comforts of childhood. Instead you are driven forward to the unknown world of adulthood. This new world might be fantastic but it could also be frightening. One thing you know for sure: It is going to be complex.

As a teen, your relationships with your parents, siblings and friends are the most treasured and complicated aspects of your life. They are a source of comfort yet confusion. At this age, you are trying to strike that exquisite balance of independence from your family while you are still dependent on them for so many things. On top of that, you are trying to decipher who is a real friend and who is not. Making things even worse, you yourself are trying on different personas, trying to figure out who you really are.

This book hopefully has helped you begin to cross that gorge with more confidence. Teens writing for teens in these pages have shared your fears, your bewilderment and your sheer exhilaration about the journey you're on and the adventures that await you. But most important, this book has shown you that even though the bridge may sway sometimes, you are not alone.

Brett Elizabeth Larkin is a junior in high school whose story, "Sara on the Wall," appears on pages 153–156.

Photo by Beth Singer

How to submit your writing, art and photos for the monthly *Teen Ink* magazine and the next *Teen Ink* book

You must be twelve to nineteen years old to be published.

- Include your name, year of birth, home address/city/ state/ZIP, telephone number and the name of your school and English teacher on each submission. Most published pieces are fewer than 2,500 words.

- Type all submissions, if possible, or print carefully in ink. We can't return any submissions, so keep a copy.

- Label all work fiction or nonfiction. Be sure to include a title.

- Affix name and address information on the back of each photo or piece of art. Please don't fold.

- Include the following originality statement in your own handwriting after each submission: "This will certify that the above work is completely original," and sign your name to affirm this is your work.

- Request anonymity. If due to the very personal nature of a piece you don't want your name published, we will respect your request, but you still must include name and address information for our records.

Other Information

If published in the magazine/book, you will receive a free copy together with a *Teen Ink* pen and a special *Teen Ink* Post-it pad.

All works submitted become the property of *Teen Ink* and all copyrights are assigned to *Teen Ink*. We retain the nonexclusive rights to publish all such works in any format. All material in *Teen Ink* is copyrighted to protect us and exclude others from republishing your work. However, all contributors retain the right to submit their work for publication elsewhere and you have our permission to do so.

Writing may be edited, and we reserve the right to publish our edited version without your prior approval.

Send all submissions to:

Teen Ink
Box 97 • Newton, MA 02461
e-mail: *Book@TeenInk.com*
phone: 617-964-6800

To learn more about the magazine and to request a free sample copy, see our Web site at *www.TeenInk.com*.

All the royalties from the sale of this book are being donated to The Young Authors Foundation

Established in 1989, The Young Authors Foundation, Inc., is the publisher of *Teen Ink* (formerly *The 21st Century*), a monthly magazine written entirely by teens for teens. This magazine has been embraced by schools and teenagers nationwide; more than 3.5 million students read *Teen Ink* magazine every year.

The magazine empowers teenagers by publishing their words, giving them a voice and demonstrating that they can make a difference. *Teen Ink* is also dedicated to improving reading, writing and critical-thinking skills while encouraging creativity and building self-esteem. The editors have read more than 300,000 submissions from students during the past twelve years, and more than 25,000 of them have been published. There is no charge to submit work, and all published contributors receive a free copy of the magazine.

In keeping with its mission, the Foundation distributes thousands of class sets and individual copies free to schools and teachers every month. In addition, more than twenty-five hundred schools support the foundation by paying a subsidized fee for their monthly class sets.

From its beginnings as a small foundation with a regional publication, The Young Authors Foundation has grown steadily and today is a national program funded with donations, sponsorships, grants and advertising from companies and individuals who support its goals. In addition to funding the magazine, the foundation under-writes a number of other educational programs:

- *Teen Ink Poetry Journal* showcases more than one thousand young poets and is distributed free to sub-scribing schools.

- *Teen Ink Educator of the Year Awards Contest* wel-comes nominating essays from students to honor outstanding teachers with cash awards, certificates and publication of their essays in the magazine.

- *Teen Ink Book Awards* program donates thousands of free books and award materials annually so schools can recognize students who have shown improvement and individual growth in the field of English.

- *Teen Ink Interview Contest* encourages thousands of teens to interview family and friends. Winners have personally interviewed national celebrities including Hillary Rodham Clinton, Colin Powell, John Glenn, Jesse Jackson, Martin Sheen, Maya Angelou and George Lucas.

- *Teen Ink Web site (www.TeenInk.com)* includes more than 13,000 pages of student writing, art, pho-tos, resources, contests and more.

The Young Authors Foundation, Inc. is a nonprofit 501(c)3 organization. See next page for details on how you can support these programs and receive a monthly copy of the magazine.

Join The Young Authors Foundation and get a monthly subscription to *Teen Ink* magazine.

Foundation Supporters Receive:
- Ten months of *Teen Ink* magazine
- Annual Newsletter
- Partner in Education Satisfaction—
  You help thousands of teens succeed.

SUPPORT TEENS' VOICES!

Only $25 per year!

The magazine includes stories, poems and art plus music, book and movie reviews, college essays, sports and more.

☐ **Annual Dues $25***
I want to receive ten monthly issues of *Teen Ink* magazine and become a supporter of The Young Authors Foundation!
(Enclose your check or complete credit card information below.)

☐ I am interested in your foundation. Please send me information about The Young Authors Foundation.

☐ I want to support the Foundation with a tax-deductible donation for $_____
(Do not send copies of the magazine.)

NAME_____PHONE _____

STREET _____

CITY/TOWN _____ STATE _____ZIP _____

PHONE_____E-MAIL _____

M/C OR VISA *(CIRCLE ONE)*#_____EXP. DATE _____/_____

Send a gift subscription to:
NAME _____

STREET_____

CITY/TOWN_____STATE_____ZIP _____

Mail coupon to: Teen Ink • Box 97 • Newton, MA 02461—Or join online: *www.TeenInk.com*

* The Young Authors Foundation, publisher of *Teen Ink*, is a 501(c)3 nonprofit organization providing opportunities for the education and enrichment of young people nationwide. While all donations support the Foundation's mission, 75% is designated for the magazine subscription, and no portion should be considered as a charitable contribution.

Acknowledgments

We want again to give special thanks to all our friends and family who have helped us make this third book in the *Teen Ink* series a reality. When we began publishing teens so long ago, back in the late 1980s, we never realized the number of amazingly talented and dedicated people who would cross our path. Many have played a large role in the overall success of our nonprofit Young Authors Foundation (which helps fund all our projects); others work with great dedication on our monthly magazine (that is the wellspring for these books); and many others support us in very special, equally important ways. We are most fortunate to have all of these people as family, friends and coworkers.

Our Children, Always First in Our Lives:

Robert Meyer, Alison Meyer Hong and her amazing husband, Michael, have always exemplified the reason we are doing this: We believe in the next generation. Their love, encouragement and wisdom have always supported us and enriched our lives.

Our Staff:

As always, thanks to our incredibly talented and always-ready-to-share-a-joke gang whose friendship and professional wisdom support us on a daily basis: Kate Dunlop Seamans, Karen Watts, Tony Abeln, as well as our long-time volunteer, Barbara Field, who has helped in many ways through the years. In addition, we appreciate the extra effort from our extended staff, which includes Paul Watts, Larry Reed and Glenn Koenig.

And an extra special thanks to our assistant editor, Denise Peck, who added her time and wisdom in helping with the final process of this book. Thanks also to Cathi Dunn MacRae whose reading and comments contributed immensely.

Our Family, Friends and Foundation Board:

Thanks to our family and friends who always offer their support on so many different levels: the Raisner gang (Barbara, Debra, Jason, David and Amy), Joseph Rice III, Jennifer and Rick Geisman, Alison Swap, Barbara Wand, Molly and Steve Dunn, Timothy Neeley, Filis Casey, Paul Chase, Paula and Lowell Fox, and Stewart and Jackie Newland. And thanks to the even larger family of Foundation Board Members: J. Robert Casey, David Anable, Richard Freedberg, as well as our Advisory Board: Beverly Beckham, Michael Dukakis, Milton Lieberman, Harold Raynolds, Susan Weld and Thomas Winship who have served with us through the years.

Our Publishing Family at HCI:

All the sensational people of HCI are always ready to help with their energy, talent and resources: Peter Vegso, the master of them all; Tom Sand, the great-idea guy; Lisa Drucker and Susan Tobias, our editors who are always ready to listen; Terry Burke and the sales group whose tireless energy helped propel the first books; Kim Weiss and Maria Dinoia; Kelly Maragni and her staff, including the amazing Randee; and, of course, Larissa Hise Henoch for her continued commitment to make the book design and graphics so creative for this entire series.

Many of these stories and poems were read and evaluated by an incredible group of students from schools across the country. Their feedback and ratings were invaluable in helping us select the final pieces for publication of this book.

Contributors

Beth Victoria Adair enjoys listening to music, reading and writing. She likes creating stories about situations that are interesting to her, and she enjoys writing about her family. Her favorite book is *The Bell Jar* by Sylvia Plath. A high-school senior, her moving story about a friend's battle with anorexia was published in *Teen Ink* magazine when she was a freshman. Beth's piece is dedicated to Sonia.

Janelle Adsit, a sophomore in high school, enjoys writing, playing the piano and singing in her school's choir. She is involved with her church, would like to travel and do missionary work. Janelle loves animals and nature and wants to own a farm. Her startling account was published in *Teen Ink* magazine last year.

Paulina Alenkina is a freshman in college. She took her photograph as a senior in high school. Although her habit of putting everything off until the last minute sometimes drives her family crazy, it's that sense of urgency she's left with that keeps her going. "Perhaps it's why I'm addicted to art and photography. There's never enough time to achieve and there's always something left."

Emily Allen graduated from college with a major in equine management. Presently, she is working in the franchise-services department of a national restaurant chain. When she's not working, Emily is involved in coaching the Special Olympics. She sketched her drawing when she was a junior in high school and says she often draws and paints as a release.

Sarah E. Allen wrote her thoughtful piece this past year as a sophomore in high school. She loves to read poetry and particularly likes the poem "Touch Me" by Stanley Kunitz. One of her favorite memories is having mashed-potato fights with her family, as well as building mashed-potato snowmen! Sarah loves spending time with her friends and playing the flute. She thanks her family for supporting her through the "crazy" teenage years and dedicates this piece to her sister, Christine.

Justin W. Avery did this somber drawing during his sophomore year in high school. Having graduated, he has parlayed his talents into a profession running his own painting business. He is also an avid skateboarder, plays the guitar and is an amateur herbalist.

Lisa Avila, a high-school senior, believes the purest act of a human being is to exercise silence. "When you are silent, you are not insulting anyone, nor are you fighting, and no harm is done." A Mexican-American, Lisa is proud to be able to speak both English and Spanish. She likes classical and pop music. Her piece is dedicated to her unique and precious family, with love.

Patrick Michael Baird took his photo using a Canon Rebel G as a senior in high school. Now a college freshman studying photography and psychology, most of his time and energy go into his school projects and photography. In his spare time he likes to visit galleries and museums and enjoy city nightlife. Patrick thanks his former photography teacher, Ms. Demetrious, for being a huge inspiration, as well as all his friends and especially his family for their support, guidance and love.

Valerie Bandura began writing because her biggest fear at five years old was growing up and not remembering what five felt like. She believes, "We write because we cannot imagine what it means not to write." A high-school junior when her piece appeared in *Teen Ink* magazine, Valerie echoes W. H. Auden, "As a rule, the sign that a beginner has a genuine original talent is that he is more interested in playing with words than in saying something original." Valerie is an M.F.A. candidate in writing.

Amber Bard is a junior at an arts high school, majoring in creative writing. She loves music and listens to many different types, including punk, jazz, reggae and classical. Amber's favorite bands are Bright Eyes, Alkaline Trio and Sublime. She enjoys writing and has created a Web site filled with stories, thoughts and ideas. In addition to writing the Preface for *Teen Ink: Friends and Family,* Amber's poem appeared in *Teen Ink* magazine this past year.

Gabrielle Rose Benadi was a high-school junior when her piece about friendship was published in *Teen Ink* magazine. Now a corporate lawyer, Gabrielle turns to poetry as her creative outlet and also enjoys reading and writing for pleasure. She dedicates her coming-of-age story to her family with appreciation and love.

Shira Bergman took this photograph of her sister for an assignment on lighting techniques. Shira credits her photography teacher, Peter Kelley, for her skills and inspiration. Now a senior in high school, Shira's favorite hobby is dancing, particularly ballet. This summer she will be a camp counselor and has been involved in a mentoring program for youngsters in her community.

Jessica L. Bethoney, a junior in high school, enjoys basketball, lacrosse, soccer, volleyball, writing and reading. She plays the piano and clarinet, and is excited to travel to Europe with her school band. Jessica's favorite times are spent hanging out with friends and family. One of her most memorable vacations was a family trip across the United States.

Kathryn Bingle wrote about her friend, "Sarah," when she was still in high school where she was active in drama club, SADD and the color guard for the band. Since then she's worked as a systems person for a large company. She is in the process of relocating to Florida where she can further enjoy outdoor activities including the seashore and sailing.

Caitlin Bird took this photograph of a young boy she was babysitting during her sophomore year of high school. Now graduated, she combines her love of photography and children as often as she can. "It's amazing how children see the world. The little boy in the picture loved the park, and I wanted to capture his enjoyment on film." Off to college in the fall, Caitlin plans to major in elementary education. She hopes to continue photography and wants to travel to England and Ireland in the next few years to take pictures.

Kimberly Blaisdell graduated from high school a year early with honors after becoming a mother. Her compelling piece about motherhood was recently published in *Teen Ink* magazine. Kimberly now attends nursing school full-time and plans to become a neonatal registered nurse. Her story is dedicated to her son, who is her "life," and her mom, who never gave up on her.

Rebecca Rae Bodfish, a recent college graduate, enjoys photography, hiking, field hockey and travel. One highlight of her life was travelling to London and all over Europe. A government major, Rebecca plans to go to law school and then settle in the Northeast. Her startling piece about her father, who has since recovered, is dedicated to her parents.

Danielle Marie Bourassa was raised speaking English and French. Her favorite place is the beach where she loves swimming and relaxing in the sun. Danielle's touching story about her relationship with her bilingual mother was published in *Teen Ink* magazine during her junior year of high school. She dedicates it to her parents and her English teacher, Mr. Marshall, who pushed his students beyond their comfort zones and helped them discover what they could accomplish. Danielle's mom is now doing fine.

Dina Cheryl Brandeis works at a major technology firm as a systems analyst and is pursuing her M.B.A. in information systems. A sophomore in high school when her touching piece was published in *Teen Ink* magazine, Dina enjoys Rollerblading, shopping, cooking and spending time with her family.

Cheryl Brewer, a college freshman, has been riding horses her entire life and wants to become a large-animal veterinarian. When she is not studying, she loves reading mysteries and scary books and writing in her journal. Cheryl worked on her high-school newspaper and was elected a "super scholar." Her story is dedicated to her "Mawmaw," the subject of this touching portrait of her grandmother, which appeared in *Teen Ink* magazine when Cheryl was a high-school senior.

Jamie Burklund, a recent high-school graduate, likes to listen to music, read, write, sleep and eat candy. Her favorite book is *White Oleander* by Janet Fitch, and her favorite movie is *American Beauty.* Jamie is a vegetarian who loves Incumbus, Fiona Apple, Tori Amos and Cat Stevens. She strongly dislikes drama queens, television, writer's block, meat, rude people and crowded hallways.

Sofiya Cabalquinto recently graduated college with a degree in English literature and creative writing. She was an editor of her college literary magazine, served as a deejay of rock and jazz shows at her college radio station, and has been published in several books, magazines and journals over the years, as well as *Teen Ink* magazine in high school. Sofiya has received numerous awards and honors for her poetry.

Nick Calcaterra has graduated from college and is now doing software consulting. His photograph was taken while he was a junior in high school. Nick can identify with the subject in his photograph. During his graduate studies, he aided other students with research, particularly in the area of river flow. After an unceremonious fall into a river in the middle of winter, Nick started his search into the warmer field of computers and software.

Joe Capolupo graduated from high school this past June and plans to pursue his love for music either during or after college. For the past five years, he has played everything from jazz to heavy metal, and is the guitarist in his band comprised of lifelong friends. They play local clubs. His amazing, totally true piece was printed in *Teen Ink* magazine this past year and is dedicated to his cousin, Christopher, who passed away last January of leukemia.

Grace Hyun Joo Chang, a sophomore in college, is studying to become a fashion designer. In high school when her artwork was published in *Teen Ink* magazine, Grace played the violin and enjoyed working on fine arts such as collages, cards and paper. She now practices digital artwork and wants eventually to design her own line of clothing. She credits her decision to become an artist to her art teacher in high school, Mrs. Sealy, and wants to thank U-myung Lee, her parents and her family.

Yoon Jeong Choe is very interested in fashion design and is pursuing a professional degree. She is always drawing and sketching and especially likes Coco Chanel, the haute couture designer. In high school, when her charcoal rendition of a table full of objects was published in *Teen Ink,* she swam on her school team and ran track. She also enjoyed tennis and volleyball and loves to sing and dance. She'd like to thank her art teacher, Mr. Mannino, the best teacher she ever had, for giving her the hope and courage to pursue her dreams.

Lollion Chong, a recent college graduate, studied for seven months in Paris on an exchange program. One of her fondest life experiences, she was able to practice French, learn a lot about fine wines and become a trained expert in the Parisian café culture. Her favorite pastime was walking along the Seine at twilight. Lollion also enjoys reading and watching films.

Sara Clark considers herself a volunteer "freak." She loves to make a difference for others in any way she can. This past summer she helped out at a women's domestic help shelter, and she does charity work through a local television station. A junior in high school, Sara would like to thank her family and her best friend Tiffany, who truly loves her for who she is.

Betsy Clauss, a recent college graduate, wants to continue studying to become a physical therapist. She enjoys Tae Bo, yoga, running and walking. Her time spent outside inspires her art. A high-school sophomore when published in *Teen Ink* magazine, Betsy recently sold her first painting and received an award for artistic achievement in her college art classes.

Amanda Coffin, a high-school senior, plays volleyball, studies martial arts and works on her school literary magazine. She waterskis and swims at her family's summer home and loves to travel. She enjoyed visiting Chile and Denmark, but her most inspiring trip was an Outward Bound program where she hiked in Colorado for two weeks.

Rachel Cohen took her photo as a freshman in high school, where she was editor of the newspaper, a member of the varsity swim team and a part-time sports correspondent for her local paper. She became senior associate sports editor in college where she also received a writing award for fiction. Graduating with a degree in public policy and English, Rachel currently works for a daily newspaper covering high-school sports.

Schuyler Coppedge has lived abroad for over two years working for an international bank after graduating from college. He has traveled throughout Europe and even Australia! In high school he enjoyed sailing and skiing, which he still pursues. He took this very interesting reflecting shot as a junior in high school where he won a number of prizes. His interest in photography has continued into adulthood.

Robert Craig is a senior in high school and took his photograph in the woods behind his home for a class assignment a couple of years ago. Still a hobby of his, he also plays lacrosse and golf for school, and does landscaping work during his summers off.

Ashley Crawford enjoys writing and dancing as a high-school senior. An emotional person, she loves any activity that allows her to express herself. Her poem is dedicated to three very special women. First, her creative-writing teacher for giving her this assignment and encouraging her to express herself freely. Next, her mom for everything, and especially for pushing her to submit this poem to *Teen Ink*. Finally, to Granny for being her inspiration and the heart behind her poem.

Michelle L. Cuevas entered college thinking she would be a theater major, but after taking an English class she realized that she wanted to write. Her classes inspire her, filling her mind with ideas that she cannot seem to get onto paper quickly enough. Michelle's piece, published in *Teen Ink* when she was a senior in high school, is dedicated to her friends and family for making her life memorable and crazy enough to write about.

Sarah Davis enjoys running, hiking, hedge laying and cross-country skiing. She was the principal French horn player in high school and won a poetry prize at college. She loves to travel and has been to Eastern and Western Europe, Taiwan, mainland China, Trans-Siberia and Britain. Her poignant poem was published in *Teen Ink* magazine during her senior year in high school. Sarah is currently pursuing a Ph.D. in medical history.

Noelle Colby DiLorenzo is a college freshman who plans to study anthropology and travel to study different cultures. She really hopes to continue her photography after taking this dramatic photo last year of her grandmother's fence (and then experimenting on the computer with it). An avid snowboarder, she also played both varsity lacrosse and soccer in high school. Noelle would like to dedicate her photo to Phil Charles, Jr.

Angie M. Drouin wrote about her grandfather when she was a senior in high school. She works in a nursing home and loves being a granddaughter to more than a hundred people! Angie enjoys life's simple pleasures including spending time with family and loved ones, cool summer-night motorcycle rides, looking at the stars and running barefoot through the grass. Her nostalgic story is dedicated to her grandfather, its inspiration.

Cera Drury had her most memorable experience learning to surf on the beaches of Southern California: feeling the sun on her back, her aching legs and the thrill of finding her balance upon crashing waves. Through this experience, she learned the value of a lesson, the pride of accomplishment and discovered her desire to teach. A junior in college, Cera's poignant piece was published in *Teen Ink* magazine when she was a high-school junior.

Thea Chapin Durling is working toward her master's degree in English as a Second Language. She is currently teaching ESL to both high-school and college students and eventually will go back to Ecuador to teach English. Her poignant account of her grandmother was published in *Teen Ink* magazine when she was a high-school sophomore. Thea would like to thank her parents for their love and support and for giving her the tools to write, and Patricio for everything.

Holly Eddy, a sophomore in college, recently became an English major to cultivate her love for writing. She works part-time to help pay for school and enjoys softball in the little free time she has. Her moving poem about leaving home, published in *Teen Ink* magazine when she was a high-school senior, is dedicated to her mother.

Carla English-Daly is a senior in college with a double major and does volunteer work with the mentally and physically challenged. "It has changed the way I look at life and shown me what's really important," she says. Carla took her photograph during her sophomore year of high school, and gives special thanks to her family and friends.

Tiffany A. Evans wrote her inspiring story about living with an alcoholic parent when she was a high-school sophomore. Now a senior in college, she is studying to become a kindergarten teacher. Tiffany is the mother of a baby girl and is in the process of planning her wedding. She dedicates her piece to her father, who has been sober for eight years. She would also like to thank her parents for making her a strong and successful woman.

Megan Farnsworth, a college junior, survived a near-fatal fall while mountain climbing last year. Although she almost had her foot amputated, camping, hiking, kayaking and canoeing are still her favorite activities. Megan believes reading and writing skills are linked, so she continues to do both as much as possible, never tackling a paper until she has learned its subject matter. Currently, her journal writing serves as her creative outlet.

Samantha Finigan, a senior in high school, shot this photo of a group of friends as part of her advanced photography class that she's taken twice because she's loved photography since junior high. An avid horseback rider who has competed in many shows, Sam's real dream is to become an actress. She's done a lot of drama in high school and is eagerly looking forward to continuing this passion in college.

Merideth Finn, a recent college graduate, is currently the director of acquisitions and production for a feature film company. This includes looking for independent films to acquire and distribute. She also searches for new filmmakers and screenwriters with whom her company can work. In her minimal spare time, she enjoys creative writing and reading. Her artwork was published in *Teen Ink* magazine when she was a high-school senior.

Karly Ford, now a sophomore in college, wrote her heart-wrenching poem as a senior in high school. At college, she loves playing rugby and participating in a comedy improv group. Combining education and comparative religion into a double major, she's traveling to Sri Lanka for a semester of study. She dedicates her poem to her mom, who now lives in Chile with her dad.

Justine M. Forrest, a high-school senior, plays lacrosse, does cheerleading, and has danced ballet, jazz and tap for twelve years. She enjoys hanging out with her friends, going to the beach and travelling. Justine spent this past summer touring all over Europe. Her favorite place is California, where she wants to attend college. Her nostalgic piece is dedicated to her father.

Sara A. Foss saw her poem celebrating summer published in *Teen Ink* magazine during her junior year in high school. She worked on her high-school and college newspapers, and was published often in her high-school literary magazine. A reporter at a major newspaper, Sara graduated from college with a major in creative writing.

Elena Fox recently graduated from college with a degree in graphic design. She plays the bass guitar, which she claims is her favorite item since it sounds beautiful and looks like rock 'n' roll. She sketched her whimsical piece as a senior in high school and wants to send a "shower of thank-yous and hugs" to her high-school art teachers, Ms. Topazio-DeMarco and Mr. Bartsch, for propelling her into a creative life and letting her take up residence in their classrooms!

Adrienne Franceschi is one of seven girls in her family! A junior in high school, she enjoys artwork and is the treasurer of her school's art club. She also loves theater and recently performed in *Little Shop of Horrors, The Children's Hour* and *The Crucible*. Adrienne works part-time as a bank teller, teaches at religious school and is a member of the National Honor Society. She thanks her best friend, Susan, for being the light of her life, and says, "Dad, this one's for you!"

Jason Friedman, a recent medical-school graduate, plans to specialize in emergency medicine. In his free time, he enjoys long-distance running (including marathons), camping, playing Ultimate Frisbee and reading. Although his piece was published in *Teen Ink* magazine a number of years ago, as a high-school senior, Jason still writes occasionally and might write a book about his final year of medical school.

Megan Galipeau shot her photo during a busy high-school AFS exchange weekend in Washington, D.C. Resting on the floor of Union Station, she looked up and was struck by the view of the staircase above her. Now a sophomore in college, she is majoring in photography and art education. She thanks her former photo teacher, Becky, for "all the encouragement and special lessons she gave me. To my Mom, Dad, sister Caycie, Mémère Noëlla and Mémère Teresa, my entire family and all the friends who supported me in my decision to attend art school, I haven't words enough to thank you for all you've given to me."

Annie Gaughen finds a writer's ability to inspire and influence others' lives incredibly exciting. She believes the greatest thing a person can do is to touch the life of another. As a high-school senior, Annie loves reading and writing, and would like to dedicate her moving account of overcoming depression to her family and her friend Becky.

Sarah Giaccai loves music, reading and traveling, and considers four months in Australia on an exchange program a major highlight of her college years. A recent graduate in communications, she wants to work for at least a year at Habitat for Humanity before pursuing graduate studies in nonprofit management. Sarah says she still takes lots of photos of "everything and anything."

Kelly Gibson loves to travel and shot this photograph at the Musée d'Orsay in Paris, which is her favorite place in the world. Kelly will start college in the fall where she'll continue to play basketball, a sport she's played since third grade. She's also been playing piano for many years. She'd like to thank her friend, Maeve, for being a patient model for her for so often, and dedicates her photography to her dad, a daily inspiration, and her late Uncle Norman, "who would have been so proud."

Jessica Griffin is a senior in high school and a member of the National Honor Society. She volunteers at a local elementary school and is on a human-rights squad. In her leisure time, Jessica loves going to major-league baseball games. Jessica has been writing since she was five years old and plans to attend college for communications. Her amusing piece is dedicated to her parents for encouraging her to write.

Tiffany Gump is a sophomore in high school where she enjoys science and history and hates French because she has a mean teacher. Tiffany is very into theater, performing in children's productions, playing the keyboard and percussion in the pit of shows and band competitions.

She would like to dedicate her hilarious remembrance to her old friends whom she hasn't seen in a while.

Elisabeth Hansen, a peer minister at her church, plans to travel around the world after college to do missionary work. A recent high-school graduate, her emotional piece was published in *Teen Ink* magazine last year. Elisabeth enjoys reading and writing, and is working on a book dedicated to her high-school friends. She also loves volleyball, classical music and visiting art museums. She reports that Torrie awoke from her coma and is recovering.

Joe Haynes, a high-school senior, plays varsity soccer, tennis and basketball. He also loves reading and writing, and compares his need to write with his need to breathe. He believes the desire to write and create is "as inborn, innate and indispensable as any other." His piece was published recently in *Teen Ink* magazine. Joe wants to study creative writing in college.

Jamie L. Heberling is a junior in college, majoring in public relations. Her most memorable experience is living in Mexico for a summer where she became fluent in Spanish and experienced other cultures and customs. Jamie enjoys travel, aerobics and keeping up with current events. Her pensive remembrance was published in *Teen Ink* magazine a few years ago when she was a high-school senior.

Erica Hebert, a recent high-school graduate, was co-editor of her school newspaper, a member of the National Honor Society and was on the school student congress. She also played field hockey, basketball and volunteered at a nursing home. As a college freshman, Erica is a print journalism major. Her piece is dedicated to her grandmother for all the fun times that inspired it.

Holly Hester is the director of marketing for a communications firm, having graduated from college. She designs advertising, direct mail and promotional materials, and conducts market research. Holly is a member of the National Sales and Marketing Council and is a licensed real-estate agent. She was a high-school sophomore when her piece was published in *Teen Ink* magazine.

Erica J. Hodgkinson was published in *Teen Ink* magazine many times during high school. Now a junior in college, she enjoys skiing, reading nonfiction and hanging around with her friends. She still enjoys photography of all kinds, although mostly she shoots black-and-white photographs. Erica took her photo as a senior in high school using a Canon EOS Rebel camera, describing the process, "I took a whole roll that day with random pictures. There wasn't anything planned."

Stephanie Hook considers herself an outspoken person who likes to be involved in many activities. She participates in Youth and Government at the local YMCA, and volunteers at Sunday school and at a children's medical center. A high-school junior, she is on the swim team and plays tennis. Stephanie loves people in general, particularly children. Her moving piece is dedicated to Jenna and Ms. Elaine and Dougie, with a special thanks to Kristen.

Jessica Hootnick is a member of the National Honor Society and is involved in peer mentoring as well as tutoring middle-school students. She is also active in her student government and the school newspaper. Captain of the school soccer team, Jessica plays on the state level, and hopes to continue her passion for soccer in college after she graduates next year.

Kathy Hufford enjoys soccer, basketball and piano. As a recent high-school graduate, she loves to travel and has been all over Europe and the United States. Kathy volunteers at an amateur radio club providing communications at local events. Her childhood account of experiencing the terror of a tornado is dedicated to her mother and, of course, Winnie-the-Pooh.

Connor Kelley graduated from high school and is beginning college this fall. During his freshman year, he almost got his big break in Hollywood when he auditioned to be an extra for a major motion picture being filmed near his hometown. Had he been chosen, he might never have taken this photo, which he dedicates to his two sisters and parents.

Lisa Kelly is on the Academic Decathlon Team, works on her school newspaper, and plays softball and soccer. She enjoys both skiing and waterskiing with her friends and family. A senior in high school, Lisa is active in her church. She would like to dedicate her funny, insightful story to her family, Kate, Shawn and her "Eleven."

Alice Kinerk was a senior in high school when her short story about fitting in was published in *Teen Ink* magazine. She is now a graduate student working toward her M.F.A. in creative writing. She hopes to move to the Northeast and become an English teacher. Alice currently works as an assistant editor of her school literary magazine.

Nathan V. Koch, a senior in high school, spends most of his time hanging out with his friends. He loves to snowboard out West, which he does all winter long, but acting is his favorite hobby. Nathan believes he is who he is because he is short. His touching, funny piece is dedicated to his sister, Amanda. Nathan believes that "without her, life would be boring."

Jaime Koniak was a junior in high school when her moving story was published in *Teen Ink* magazine. Currently attending law school, Jaime has won several writing awards. She has worked for *Rolling Stone* magazine and the *Atlanta Business Chronicle*. Her piece is dedicated to her grandma, who taught her the value of quiet strength and unconditional love.

Val Koutmina was born in Russia and speaks the language at home. A high-school junior, she enjoys hanging out with her friends, visiting other towns, relaxing in coffee shops and writing. Val likes playing soccer and lacrosse and taking care of animals. Writing is her outlet to express all the beauty she has felt and the excitement of each day. Her poem is dedicated to all those who surround her, friends and enemies alike, who help create the joy or heartbreak that fuel her creative spirit.

Holly M. Kuczynski, a high-school senior, enjoys many activities, including horseback riding, painting, reading, listening to music, going to shows, meeting new people, writing and reading. Francesca Lia Block is her favorite author. Holly's piece is dedicated to anyone who has struggled with self-acceptance or eating disorders and to those who stand by them. She says to remember that, "Hope can sometimes be misplaced, but it is never truly lost."

Katrina Lahner recently wrote this amazing piece recalling a memorable incident with her father. Having just graduated from high school, she plans to continue her education at a university in the fall.

Steven Lam wrote his insightful poem as a senior in high school, where he enjoyed his writing class and played violin in the orchestra. Currently a college sophomore, he has made many friends. Originally in the engineering school where he loved studying computers, he is trying to choose a major. He works in the summers, sometimes at his family's restaurant.

Patrick Lane, a college freshman, plays soccer, tennis and guitar. He fondly remembers those three magical summers in Lenox, Massachusetts, where he visited Edith Wharton's old mansion, the subject of his thoughtful piece. Patrick plans to work on his college newspaper and someday become a writer.

Brett Elizabeth Larkin wrote her first "novel" at the age of six and has been hooked on writing ever since. As a junior in high school, she says, "My stories insist that I write them! Story ideas nag me throughout the school day and as I try to fall asleep. There's no rest until I succumb and write the ideas down. I believe a good work of fiction is like fine art: It serves as a mirror that reflects and a prism that refracts ideas from every angle." Brett also loves acting, tennis and dance.

Brianna Lee loves the arts and has a passion for Broadway. She hopes to live in New York City where she can be at the center of it all. As a junior in high school, she takes writing very seriously and has been practicing since childhood, and may become a journalist. Her favorite idea? To "think happy thoughts." Her hilarious story was recently published in *Teen Ink* magazine.

Janine B. Lee wrote her piece as a senior in high school where she was news editor of a science publication, a researcher at a laboratory and a national finalist for a science prize. Currently, Janine is a junior in college studying premedicine. She volunteers as a mentor/tutor at a junior high school.

Christine Loftus, a recent high-school graduate, is a singer and pianist in a local band. She loves to write music and lyrics, and dreams of touring worldwide with her band. Christine plans to go to college for music education and voice, and eventually settle in London. Her poetry is inspired by what she believes inspires everyone: art and emotion.

Danielle Lukowski finally had her braces removed after two years, then had a car accident where she lost her front tooth and had to get braces all over again! Despite this, she says her biggest reality check was when she won a critics choice award for a short fiction piece and the judge asked why she had never before been published, he declared, "You're just lazy." A senior in high school, Danielle dedicates her story to him. "I'll never be lazy again!"

Amanda J. Luzar took this photograph during her junior year of high school. She recently graduated and begins college in the fall. Amanda was born in Germany and lived in Singapore for some time before moving to America three years ago. She would like to thank her model in the photo, Lisa, and her dog, Gypsie.

Jennifer Maberry once only wrote for school assignments, but began enjoying it so much that she decided to do it all the time. She also likes playing soccer and volunteering, particularly with children. A recent high-school graduate, Jennifer plans to study nursing in college and then work with children with terminal illnesses. Her piece is dedicated to her dad for showing her what it means to be truly happy.

Erienne McCoole works at a camera store in order to learn more about the technical aspects of her love, photography. A senior in high school, she wants to go to art school and pursue this passion full-time. Erienne dreams of returning to Italy, where she went once on a school trip and traveled around Rome, Venice and the countryside taking photographs. She thanks all of her teachers, especially her three travelling companions.

Mary-Helena McInerney, a sophomore in college, is studying to become a psychologist and an author. She enjoys reading new-age fiction and nonfiction, particularly the works of James Redfield, and wants to write her own philosophical novel someday. Mary-Helena practices holistic healing therapies, meditation and Tai Chi. She has a pet iguana named Tool.

Dan Feng Mei enjoys reading, writing, listening to music and singing. During her last two years of high school, she was a semi-finalist in the Intel Science Search. Dan Feng enjoys working with and teaching children. A college sophomore, her heartfelt piece about her mother was published in *Teen Ink* magazine during her senior year of high school.

Lisa Miles is a college freshman who plans to become an architect, as her father was. She has recently discovered her love of the visual arts, and has won many awards. She also loves horses and many outdoor activities. One of her favorite places is her hammock, especially during a storm. Growing up without her dad for the past six years, she and her four brothers and two sisters are very close ("almost"). She now has four and a half nephews and one and a half nieces, all of whom she adores. She would like to dedicate her poignant piece (published in *Teen Ink* last year) to her daddy.

Holly Miller is involved in her student council and the prom planning committee as a senior in high school. She also enjoys playing the piano. Holly works at an interior-design school and volunteers at a children's museum. Her nostalgic poem was recently published in *Teen Ink* magazine.

Jordana Mishory, a college freshman majoring in journalism, plans to get a Ph.D. in psychology. She enjoys reading, writing poetry, tap dancing and volunteering in her free time. Jordana was a member of Key Club and chaired her community-service club in high school. She wrote and directed a play for children and wants to write screenplays. Her piece is dedicated to Sonya, who hasn't minded her being "weird" for the past ten years.

Karen M. Moran was first published in *Teen Ink* magazine when she was a senior in high school. She has since graduated from college and wants to become a high-school sociology or English teacher. She thinks the teenage years are interesting because of the many life-changing experiences that occur. Karen's poem was written for her mom, who passed away when she was five.

Jennifer Morisson, a recent college graduate, wants to teach elementary-school music. A percussionist in her college concert band and a student conductor, Jennifer also teaches piano. She is a vegetarian as well as an animal-rights activist. One of her favorite experiences was spending a semester studying music and Italian in Milan, Italy.

Kerri Lynn Morrone was published in *Teen Ink* magazine as a high-school sophomore. A recent college graduate, Kerri received her B.A. in English. She achieved many honors and leadership opportunities, and boasts of owning a calico cat who can sit and fetch!

Elizabeth A. Moseman spent her senior year of high school in Germany as an exchange student. She travelled throughout Europe and even Sri Lanka. Published in *Teen Ink* magazine during her senior year of high school, she is now a college sophomore majoring in environmental studies. Liz spent her summer living on a desolate Caribbean island, helping a Ph.D. student conduct research on an endangered bird. Her beautiful poem is dedicated to her mother and grandmother.

Lindsay Moss has two passions: language and waitressing. She cannot wait to see where she ends up in life, but she focuses on enjoying the present moment. She loves eating Hershey's chocolate and going to a new cineplex near her home. A junior in high school, Lindsay's insightful poem appeared in *Teen Ink* magazine this year.

Peter Kelly Muller, a sophomore in college, decided to travel around Europe this year and experience different cultures. He believes there is no better way to learn about yourself and your own country than to see other lands. His mother is his greatest inspiration. He thanks her for always being there.

Laurel L. Oberg served on her high-school student council and was voted an outstanding representative. Now a sophomore in college, she serves on the student congress and received a special award for her leadership abilities. Laurel wrote her touching piece about her grandfather as a high-school senior.

Susan E. Ogar worked for a magazine in London while travelling through Europe taking lots of photographs after she graduated from college. Now the marketing director at a publishing company, she still enjoys photography and writes whenever she can. During high school, Susan ran her school darkroom, was the photo editor of her school yearbook, played field hockey and excelled at creative writing.

Cassie Olsen entered college as a theater major, but decided to pursue biology instead. She would like to contribute to the field of medicine and is incredibly excited about her future. A college sophomore, her poem was published in *Teen Ink* magazine when she was a high-school senior. Cassie dedicates it to those who believe there is no light at the end of the tunnel—"There is; hang in there."

Kelley Pastyrnak, a high-school junior, wants to attend college and become an English teacher. She is passionate about dance, which she has studied since she was three years old. She also loves reading and writing, and writes to express her innermost thoughts and feelings. Her poignant memoir is dedicated to her mother—her best friend and inspiration.

Patricia Pelczar wrote her thought-provoking piece as a senior in high school. Currently pursuing a Ph.D. in microbiology, she hopes to become a college professor. Patricia loves watching and playing sports and going to the gym. She also adores horseback riding and has competed in shows for many years. Family has always been incredibly important to Patricia, and she believes they have helped her become who she is.

Johna Phillips is a sophomore in high school. A lover of animals, Johna and her family live on a ranch where she has many pets. She plays volleyball and loves traveling to Arizona to visit her grandparents. Johna dedicates her drawing to her "beautiful, wonderful mother, Jeani."

Annette K. Pollert is a college sophomore majoring in English and art history. A senior in high school when her poem was published in *Teen Ink* magazine, Annette was editor-in-chief of her high-school newspaper, on the German Club board, and helped teach foreign language in local elementary schools. Annette enjoys attending lectures and poetry readings, painting watercolors and sailing.

Sierra Pope, a high-school sophomore, loves the outdoors and all kinds of writing. She might like to be an English teacher, since her eighth-grade English teacher is her inspiration. With big goals, Sierra says, "I will climb a mountain, write a book and save the world." Her piece, which appeared earlier this year in *Teen Ink,* is dedicated to her younger brother, Ian.

Nicole K. Press has done gymnastics for as long as she can remember and currently teaches it to children. She also volunteers at the Special Olympics. Nicole enjoys reading, writing, photography and being a techie for theater productions. She would like to design sets professionally. A senior in high school, her insightful poem was published in *Teen Ink* magazine this past year.

Kimberly Burke Reilly was a high-school senior when her nostalgic account was published in *Teen Ink* magazine. She recently received a master's degree in the history of decorative arts and is working as a consultant and appraiser of antique furniture and decorative arts. She thanks her parents for all the great times and experiences they've shared.

Lexie Rich, a high-school junior, loves dancing, music, running track and going to the beach. Having always loved reading poetry and short stories, she often also writes poems and philosophical essays. Lexie wants to become a writer or an accountant since she loves numbers and math. Her remembrance of a special night is dedicated to her best friend, Krista.

Jana Richardson, a junior in college, loves theater and performed this poignant piece about her grandfather in an acting class. She also enjoys reading, writing, running and volunteering as a tutor. Jana plans to visit Cape Town, South Africa, for a semester to study history. Her piece was published in *Teen Ink* magazine when she was a senior in high school.

Alison Riley graduated college as an English major. She enjoys knitting, refinishing furniture and writing short stories. A high-school senior when her piece was published in *Teen Ink* magazine, Alison works as a graphic designer because it allows her the time to read, write and remember.

Laura Robichaux, a high-school senior, has been dancing for more than fourteen years. Despite recent knee surgery, her life revolves around her lessons and school. Laura also participates in student council and honors council. In her spare time, she likes to be with friends and have fun. She thanks her family and close friends for their support.

David Rochelson, a freshman in college interested in writing, was the co-editor of his school newspaper, directed two one-act plays, acted in a local theater group and played volleyball. A frequent contributor to *Teen Ink,* his thoughtful short story appeared this past year. David thanks his parents for their support, his brothers for making him laugh, his writing teacher for applauding him when he was right and for making him see when he was wrong, and finally, Harriet.

Valerie Ross enjoys spending time with friends, writing poetry, learning theatrical scripts and studying Japanese. Her favorite places are Acadia National Park and Scotland because of their magnificent scenery. Valerie would like to thank Bill Littell, who not only convinced her to submit her writing for publication, but challenged her to write pieces she was proud of. A sophomore in high school, her story was recently published in *Teen Ink* magazine.

Nicholas Ruggiero, a high-school junior when his photograph was published in *Teen Ink* magazine, works as a software analyst with a technology company. He wants to get his M.B.A. and develop some of his own product ideas. Nicholas plays the piano, practices martial arts and works out often. He loves to travel and would like to become proficient in another language. His photo is dedicated to his parents.

Audrey Rutledge did her drawing this year as a junior in high school. She is very active and enjoys running, working out and riding horses. "I feel blessed to have such a great life, and I think the things I love are reflected in my artwork." She dedicates this drawing to her mother and father.

Ranika Sanchez is on her school's cheerleading squad and participates in youth choir at her church. A high-school junior, she loves Florida and hopes to attend college there. One memorable experience was attending a fellowship of Christian athletes, where she met many people and learned more about her religion. Ranika would like to thank her parents and family for guiding her through everything, and her friends for their constructive criticism.

Matt Schafer only works in black-and-white photography, and although he's been doing it as long as he can remember, he says it is just a hobby. This photograph was taken while Matt was still in junior high school. He is currently a freshman in high school and enjoys being on both the football and tennis teams.

Alexa Schuler, a college sophomore, is on her school swim team. An elementary-education major, she likes skateboarding and taking pictures in her free time. Alexa thanks Mr. Kelley for making photography more fun than any other teacher ever has. She was published in *Teen Ink* magazine numerous times during high school.

Amanda Sengstacken, a high-school junior, is a member of the English honor society. She has studied ballet and modern dance for more than ten years and often performs in productions. She enjoys art and design, and would like to become an architect. Amanda volunteers at a children's ward of a hospital. Her emotional poem about her grandmother was published in *Teen Ink* magazine this year.

Joelle M. Shabat is an officer of SADD, teaches Hebrew school, tutors a child and works part-time. Her most treasured possessions are her teddy bear, an autographed Metallica T-shirt and a mother-child necklace that was her mom's. Joelle loves to read, write, be with her friends, shop, practice black-and-white photography and travel. A senior in high school, Joelle would like to dedicate this piece to Adam, an integral part of her life.

Dana C. Silano has been creating poetry and fiction for as long as she can remember. She writes to vent her emotions and often re-reads her journals to see how she has progressed. Dana's insightful poem was published in *Teen Ink* magazine when she was a high-school junior. Now a sophomore in college majoring in journalism, her poem is dedicated to her best friend, her mother.

Rebecca Silverman is enjoying her sophomore year in high school. She writes, "Some people say sophomore year is the worst because you're not new, but you're not yet an upperclassman—kind of in-between. I think it's only the worst if you make it the worst, because I'm having a great time." Rebecca is active with youth leadership and diversity programs both in and out of school. She also plays the piano and hopes to continue studying photography in the future. Rebecca dedicates her photo to her friend, Rachel, who was playing around on an old jungle gym when she shot her photograph last year.

B. J. Simmons, a college freshman, loves writing poems and short stories. A fan of Edgar Allen Poe, he loves to read and particularly enjoys horror stories and "twisted tales." B. J. also likes music and discovered his passion for writing through penning song lyrics. He wants to become a professional writer and thanks his friends and family for their support.

Beth Singer credits her high-school photography teacher for her formal training, but was also fortunate to be able to learn some professional techniques from her cousins who are magazine photographers. She took these pictures in her senior year and heads off to college this fall.

Stephen Siperstein has had his photographs exhibited in a local arts festival, where he also won an essay contest. He is a senior in high school and a musician "to the core." He has been playing the guitar and piano for years, and has even taught children how to play. This summer he will work as a camp counselor. He shoots primarily black-and-white photographs and was a finalist in a national photo contest for *Photographer's Forum Magazine.*

Katelyn M. Smith is on the debate team, runs track and cross country, and works on her school newspaper. She also works at a small sub shop and at a day camp for four- to six-year-olds in the summer. A junior in high school, Katelyn likes vacationing in New England. She dedicates her nostalgic piece to her mom.

Kellie Smith and her family own boarding stables where they house and care for twelve horses. She is an avid rider and has been showing for the last two years. Kellie, now a senior, took this photograph as a junior and is excited to have a venue where teenagers can share their art and ideas with other teens.

Pam Smykal is a senior in high school and a member of the school crew team. She recently enjoyed a trip to Spain and now hopes to study abroad while in college. Pam dedicates her moving story to "all of the friends who walk in when the rest of the world walks out."

Josh Stadtlander-Miller, a senior in high school, participates in track and Model UN, and volunteers three days a week for his state's assemblyperson. He plays piano and locarina (a small flute-like instrument), and loves playing video games. He thanks his brother for inspiring him, and dedicates his piece to everyone he knows, especially his beloved grandparents.

Natalie R. Studwell, a college junior, is majoring in vocal performance. Although she is primarily focused on music, she also enjoys writing and contributes to her school newspaper. Natalie works as a desk aide and enjoys volunteer work when she has time. Her poem, published in *Teen*

Ink magazine when she was a high-school senior, is dedicated to Chris, a constant source of inspiration and support.

Christine Susienka has always known what she wants to be when she grows up. She has first-grade papers with "I want to be a writer" scrawled on them, and has always loved words. She is inspired by the profound effect they can have on people and wants to use her writing to make a difference. A junior in high school, Christine thanks her parents for their support and encouragement.

Hannah R. Tadros wrote her personal account as a senior in high school where she was president of the literary and the multicultural clubs. Coordinator of the Bible study group, her interest has continued in college where she participates in the intervarsity Christian club. She plans a double major in journalism and management and still enjoys writing nonfiction. An Egyptian by birth, she has lived in the United States since she was quite young.

Nicholas Taylor, now a college junior, saw his moving poem published in *Teen Ink* magazine when he was a high-school sophomore. He plans to attend graduate school to become an English professor and write about the American rock and music culture. His writing is inspired by the exuberance, romanticism and freedom of the Beat Generation. Nicholas works for his school newspaper as well as interning at a local newspaper.

Elizabeth Torpey is an English teacher at an all-boys high school. Since she's always treasured female friendships and has explored the ways in which young women wrestle with issues of identity and self-worth through writing, Elizabeth is fascinated by the natural humor of teenage boys and wants to write about her teaching experiences. Elizabeth's insightful reflections on her adoption were published when she was a junior in high school. Since then, she has actually met her birth mother.

Amanda Jill Turkanis is very active as a junior in high school, playing varsity soccer and being involved in student government as class president. Since the age of three, she also has been a student of dance, including ballet, jazz, musical theater, tap and acrobatics! Amanda spends a lot of time volunteering at a local shelter for abused women. She would like to thank her parents and brothers for all their love and support.

Tiffany Turner took this photograph of her brother, Brandon, for a class assignment in double exposure. She dedicates it to her art teacher, Mrs. Lowe. Tiffany also loves to paint and draw and is active in an art society within her school. A junior in high school, she's involved in soccer, track and drama. She's finishing a historical novel for which she hopes to find a publisher.

Kelly J. Van Deusen enjoys volunteering with those who have challenges. She likes writing personal essays, hanging out with friends and painting. Kelly works part-time at a florist, which she loves because she gets to make people happy. Her favorite movie is *Clueless* because she can understand where the characters are coming from. Kelly, a college freshman, wants to study advertising. She thanks her friends and family who are always an inspiration.

Joanne Wang, a junior in college, loves to read, write, have good conversations, eat Rocky Road ice cream and laugh. She is involved in Christian Fellowship and tutors students in her spare time. She believes she will meet her future husband in a bookstore or library because she has a weakness for intellectual types. Joanne thanks her dear friend, Stephanie, who is always an inspiration. Her poignant piece was published in *Teen Ink* magazine last year.

Matt Wiesenfeld considers himself "a pretty average guy." A junior in high school, he never realized writing was a strength until he was published a few times in *Teen Ink* magazine. Matt participates on his school baseball, basketball and track teams. His story is dedicated to his grandpa.

Janna Jae Wilber, a college sophomore, plans to major in education to teach math in middle school because she's good at it. She loves college and has joined the swimming team. *Teen Ink* published her remembrance when she was a senior in high school where she was active in drama, performing in many musicals. She also enjoyed the outing club, which she has continued in college. She dedicates her piece to Jenny and Laura with whom she is still friends, returning to that rock yearly.

Emily H. Wilson, currently a college sophomore, is majoring in education with a minor in Spanish. She enjoys writing stories that analyze people's feelings in different situations. She loves working with children and wants to become an elementary-school teacher. Emily, whose startling short story appeared this past year, would like to thank her father for being so supportive.

Josh Winslow graduated from college as an economics major and now works in sales at a mutual-fund company. He spends his free time sailing, skiing, biking and rock climbing. He and his fiancée recently biked across Alaska in a benefit ride and plan to participate in future bike trips for charity. Published in *Teen Ink* magazine as a high-school sophomore, Josh enjoys reading, particularly history books, and still writes fiction for fun.

Cecilia Woodworth, a junior in high school, was inspired to write her heartfelt poem, which recently appeared in *Teen Ink* magazine, when she went on a mission trip to Honduras. Although she was there to help people, they ended up helping her learn about herself. Cecilia wants to share the blessings of her life with others. She loves reading and writing, being creative and being with her friends. She wants to thank her cat, Ada Leah, who never gets mad at her and always cheers her up.

Mary H. Wu started writing when she was ten to cope with the pain of her kidney problems and because she wanted to be a great writer just like her sister. Now a sophomore in college, Mary wrote her uplifting story about friendship when she was a senior in high school. She thanks her dad, TC, and, of course, her best friend, Jennifer.

Stacey Zabusky was published in *Teen Ink* magazine as a high-school senior. Now a college sophomore majoring in family studies, Stacey hopes to work with children. She is a sorority member and enjoys shopping, talking, reading and travel. She wants to study in London and visit different parts of Europe. Her account of those weekly family dinners is dedicated to her parents who instilled strong values by taking the time to have that weekly family dinner, even if she didn't always appreciate it.

Danielle Zonghi plays the piccolo, flute, piano and bass guitar. She loves to listen to ska and punk music, and was the stage manager for her school drama club. Danielle will enter college this fall to study music and business. Her emotional piece is dedicated to her father; his "afterglow" shines on her family every day.

Permissions *(continued from page vi)*

"Maybe Tomorrow." Reprinted by permission of Kelly J. Van Deusen. ©2001 Kelly J. Van Deusen.

"Girl in Light and Shadow." Reprinted by permission of Amanda J. Luzar. ©2001 Amanda J. Luzar.

"I Wish." Reprinted by permission of Mary-Helena McInerney. ©1996 Mary-Helena McInerney.

"Almost a Sister." Reprinted by permission of Stephanie Hook. ©2001 Stephanie Hook.

"Somewhere." Reprinted by permission of Cecilia Woodworth. ©2001 Cecilia Woodworth.

"Peter Rabbit Wore Wool." Reprinted by permission of Jana Richardson. ©1997 Jana Richardson.

"Seeds We Sow." Reprinted by permission of B. J. Simmons. ©2000 B. J. Simmons.

"Red Guilt." Reprinted by permission of Holly Hester. ©1991 Holly Hester.

"Sea of Green." Reprinted by permission of Katrina Lahner. ©2001 Katrina Lahner.

"Woman Sniffing Flowers." Reprinted by permission of Grace Hyun Joo Chang. ©1995 Grace Hyun Joo Chang.

"Neighbor Friend." Reprinted by permission of Valerie Bandura. ©1991 Valerie Bandura.

"Portrait of Young Girl." Reprinted by permission of Carla English-Daly. ©1998 Carla English-Daly.

"Apple Pie." Reprinted by permission of Dina Cheryl Brandeis. ©1993 Dina Cheryl Brandeis.

"I Had a Bad Time." Reprinted by permission of Alice Kinerk. ©1996 Alice Kinerk.

"A Glance in the Mirror." Reprinted by permission of Kelley Pastyrnak. ©2000 Kelley Pastyrnak.

"Omar, Are You Sleeping?" Reprinted by permission of Sofiya Cabalquinto. ©1996 Sofiya Cabalquinto.

"Out of Focus Guy." Reprinted by permission of Peter Kelly Muller. ©2001 Peter Kelly Muller.

"The Black Bandanna." Reprinted by permission of Joe Capolupo. ©2001 Joe Capolupo.

"A Quiet Enemy." Reprinted by permission of Beth Victoria Adair. ©1999 Beth Victoria Adair.

"Girl Looking Down." Reprinted by permission of Patrick Michael Baird. ©2000 Patrick Michael Baird.

"She Tried." Reprinted by permission of Dana C. Silano. ©1999 Dana C. Silano.

"Another Step Closer." Reprinted by permission of Janelle Adsit. ©2000 Janelle Adsit.

"Man's Face." Reprinted by permission of Justin W. Avery. ©1994 Justin W. Avery.

"Watching Her." Reprinted by permission of Holly Eddy. ©1999 Holly Eddy.

"The Journal." Reprinted by permission of Joelle M. Shabat. ©2001 Joelle M. Shabat.

"The Balcony." Reprinted by permission of Hannah R. Tadros. ©2000 Hannah R. Tadros.